THE
PUPPET
MASTER
OF
ISLAM

A Fabricated Religion

RICHARD BENNETT

LifeRich Publishing is a registered trademark of The Reader's Digest Association, Inc.

LifeRich Publishing books may be ordered through booksellers or by contacting:

LifeRich Publishing
1663 Liberty Drive
Bloomington, IN 47403
www.liferichpublishing.com
844-686-9607

Because of the dynamic nature of the Internet, any web addresses or links contained in this book may have changed since publication and may no longer be valid. The views expressed in this work are solely those of the author and do not necessarily reflect the views of the publisher, and the publisher hereby disclaims any responsibility for them.

Any people depicted in stock imagery provided by Getty Images are models, and such images are being used for illustrative purposes only. Certain stock imagery © Getty Images.

Back cover photo by Paula Richards

Scripture quotations marked (NIV) are taken from the Holy Bible, New International Version®, NIV®. Copyright © 1973, 1978, 1984, 2011 by Biblica, Inc.™ Used by permission of Zondervan. All rights reserved worldwide. www.zondervan.com The "NIV" and "New International Version" are trademarks registered in the United States Patent and Trademark Office by Biblica, Inc.™

Scripture taken from the New King James Version®. Copyright © 1982 by Thomas Nelson. Used by permission. All rights reserved.

Scripture quotations taken from the New American Standard Bible® (NASB), Copyright © 1960, 1962, 1963, 1968, 1971, 1972, 1973, 1975, 1977, 1995 by The Lockman Foundation Used by permission. www.Lockman.org

ISBN: 978-1-4897-4251-3 (sc)
ISBN: 978-1-4897-4250-6 (hc)
ISBN: 978-1-4897-4252-0 (e)

Library of Congress Control Number: 2022911322

Print information available on the last page.

LifeRich Publishing rev. date: 08/19/2022

They came, they saw, they almost conquered.

Contents

Introduction ix

I   Inside Islam… 1

II   The Conception of Islam 7

III   Pre Islam—Zoroastrianism 15

IV   The Slaughter at Medina 20

V   Sunni & Shiite Differences 32

VI   The Women of Islam 37

VII   R-Rated Brutality 43

VIII The Other Guys 48

IX   The Proven Intent of Islam 55

X   Merciless Avengers 60

XI   Number of Merciless Avengers 66

XII   Can Jihad be Justified? 70

XIII   The Removal of Peace 79

XIV   A Protected Chattel 85

XV   Two (Three) Gods, One Space 96

XVI   Islamic Rewards 105

XVII Are We Foolish People? 111

XVIII Political Correctness 120

XIX   Are We Islamophobic? 127

XX   Governed by Sharia Law 140

XXI   The Head of The Dragon 156

XXII The Terrorist Next Door 168

XXIII The Deception of Islam 176

XXIV The Dilemma of Peace 185

XXV Post Letter Warnings 197

XXVI The Reuniting of The Jews 209

XXVII The Some Parting Words 216

Introduction

IMPORTANT NEWS OF THE DAY, how long will it be important news is anyone's guess. In addition to the constant threat of Islam bringing another 9/11 to our doorstep, and China threating war over Taiwan, we read daily about how Russia is busy invading Ukraine. While enduring tens of thousands of strangers, some friendly some not, entering our country monthly, all during the time we are dealing with a pandemic. And according to some, perhaps one of many pandemics that will be coming down the pike. A pike, that is bringing us to the point of asking ourselves many questions.

Some of the questions might involve the latest government requirements. Are we wearing masks? Have we received our vaccination? Should we get vaccinated? Is this becoming a war between the vaccinated and unvaccinated? On and on it goes, Democrats against Republicans, Republicans against Democrats, brother against brother and so on. Our country has never been as divided as it is right now. And this is not even considering the threat Islam poses, but we know that. Just looking around confirms the reality of what was just said.

A quote you might find interesting comes from Jack Van Impe as he quoted Dr. Martin Luther King Jr., who said, "Nothing in the world is more dangerous than sincere ignorance and conscientious stupidity." To that I believe we can only say, it's as if America, perhaps as well as the rest of the world, stepped into the twenty-first century with a terminal case of both. Even now our Supreme Court is under attack for some decisions they are making. When did America stop understanding it is impossible to please everyone? AND that is creating a problem. Regardless of which way the country goes, everyone knows their will be unrest, both physically and mentally.

It is as if overnight the world has reached the place where many are equating current conditions to those mentioned in the Bible as the end times, the last days before the coming of Christ, and pointing to the Bible for conformation. Or, as a Muslim would say, the coming of al Mahdi, and pointing to the Quran for conformation. Are we as close to the "last of days" as many Christians seem to be bringing to our attention? We will have to wait and see is all most can say. That is also, all anyone can say about Islam, we will have to wait and see.

For those who bet, the smart money is on Islam bringing destruction to our shores as they have in the past, especially since Iran is home to the Iranian Republican Guard, a brutal terrorist organization who now has control of Afghanistan that spawns the Taliban (a brutal, fundamentalist religious group). Twenty years we were there. Twenty years of sacrifice and what does America have to show for it? But more importantly, did we learn from it? After thousands of lives lost and trillions of dollars spent, we are inviting the enemy we were unable to stop in their country, into our country. Am I wrong? This book illustrates the pending disaster from such decisions.

Only in America could an enemy of the State be elected to governmental positions as Muslims are, so that they can continue to promulgate their ideology of what Islam, especially Sharia law, brings to the table. Most Americans understand we have differences but during these peaceful moments many might ignore some of the more dangerous differences. What they are ignoring is the fact that it is Islam's destiny to defeat and destroy the American way of life. And when Americans try to discuss the differences, we are besmirched with insults. I should have titled this book, "Goodbye America—Hello Islam." Or "Goodbye America—hello Secularism." It is as if one or the other is destined to take down the America we know.

Many might take offense to this book just as they took offense to Joel Richardson's book, *The Islamic Messiah,* as it reveals much about Islam that exist beneath the surface. A place as defined by their literature as well as their teachings and their actions. Much of which reveals the mind of a Muslim. And when that information is opened for discussion, many say, they are misunderstood or perhaps we must pray for them to accept Christ.

Personally, I can say that I have never met a Muslim I didn't like, but that doesn't change the fact that we see things differently. Does that make us good and them bad? Of course not, but it is impossible to ignore the fact that Islam brings a lot of brutality to the table. And because of this perception, many might begin describing Islam by saying; Plane's crash, people get hurt, American flags are burned and the nation of Islam praises Allah. Followed by the question: Why is that?

Well, the response to that question would depend upon who was asked. As we might expect, Christians would answer it differently than a Muslim. For example, in answering that question, a Muslim would probably avoid saying; "If the truth be known, eliminating the Christian God, and those who acknowledge him, is part of our destiny." We have that straight from an Islamic Iman. Eliminating the creator God and replacing him with the god introduced into the world by a night vision is what many Muslims live and die for—literally.

Most know Islam is not averse to retaliation when they think they have been wronged. I was thinking, I don't believe one could alienate a few million Muslims any quicker than to begin a book titled; The Puppet Master of Islam—A Fabricated Religion. It would be virtually the same if a book was released titled; The Puppet Master of Christianity—A Fabricated Religion. I believe many would take some issue either way. However, while one might complain, disapprove of, and even protest—let us put them in the Christian camp, the other might think of eliminating the messenger, let's put them in the Islamic camp.

What you are about to read would be considered unbelievable by many, and yet it is true. It seems as if anyone speaking out against Islam, or it's initiators, Muhammad or Allah, is putting a death sentence upon his or her life. The threat of death is not unrealistic. There was a recent event that occurred in France where many people lost their life because of a drawing of Muhammad. Denmark published cartoons of Muhammad sometime back and some of the fallout from that incident included more than 130 Christians in the Nigerian cities of Maiduguri and Onitsha being slaughtered by Muslims and six children being burned to ashes in front of their fathers.

What advances Islam to the place they are destined, is acceptable to Islam, and the Muslim community in general. Then conversely, what adversely portrays Islam is cause for death. Sometime back Joel Richardson wrote a book titled *The Islamic Antichrist.*[1] A book that caused the author to receive many death threats just for exposing some truths about Islam. He chose the following email of the many to be included in his book. The email went as follows:

> I will chop off your head! May Allah damn you and your whole family. May you and your whole family all rot in hell forever. I want you to know that all Muslims call upon Allah to damn you and put you in hell. I will personally kill you. I will personally kill your family. You will die a very slow and painful death *inshallah* (by the will of Allah)."

---

[1] Joel Richardson. *The Islamic Antichrist.* World Net Daily. Los Angeles, CA. 2009. A personal thanks to Joel for granting me permission to use the information.

It was shortly after receiving this email that Joel wrote about his thoughts. He said it was not the only email that he had received, but it was the one that caused him to begin practicing quite a bit more discretion in his interactions with Muslims in the context of interfaith dialogue. Others have retracted, recanted, or renounced any criticism of Islam when the reality of Islam came knocking.

Why? Why would anything written offend anyone to the point it would warrant death? There is only one answer: What has been written in this book, as well as in Joel's book, is the revelation (exposure) of the powers behind the "spirits of Islam." Spirits that have been unleashed upon the world, allowing for the introduction of a different god, a god many consider to be a fabricated god. A god to deceive approximately 1.3 billion individuals.

As never before, the information you are about to read exposes Islam for what it really is and exposes the beliefs of those who follow Muhammad and bow to Allah. I would say for the most part, this book is not about what one sees manifested on the surface, but as mentioned, what goes on beneath the surface where Allah lives.

I

Inside Islam...

...AN AWAKING: WHEN ONE DISCUSSES the inside of Islam, they are introduced to a religion that is quite different than any other religion and a god that is quite different from any other God, especially the God of Christians. The Islamic god has great ambitions with perhaps the greatest being, to overthrow and eventually eliminate the God who orchestrated history from Geneses to Revelation—the "I Am" God of the burning bush. The God who told Isaiah, "Before me no God was formed, nor will there be one after me." (Isaiah 43:10, NIV). Christians accept that while Islam makes that out to be a fabrication. After saying that, they claim, both Muslims and Christians worship and serve one God. Do we? That will be an interesting topic of discussion later.

The first time I saw the meaning or perhaps the results of Islam was when Juan Williams, a former commentator for NPR was fired for just being honest. It was while boarding a plane and observing a couple of Iman's boarding the same plane that he made a comment. He said he gets nervous when boarding a plane and seeing Muslims in full Islamic attire. He's probably not alone when he feels this way, but he was perhaps the only one fired for expressing feelings regarding those who have said repeatedly, they want to do us harm, those who have said they want to eliminate us, kill us, otherwise remove us from this world any way possible.

Would I be considered Islamophobic for stating that, even though it is a fact? For those who perhaps missed what Muslims have been saying for the last fourteen hundred years, especially Muslims who accept Muhammad as a prophet and Allah as a God,

1

then listen-up perhaps we can play a little catch-up. It comes as no surprise that radical Islamic Muslims want to eliminate us, at least that is what they tell us…repeatedly. What does come as somewhat of a surprise is the fact that most Americans only see the good in Muslims and do not consider the dangerous ideology they follow.

I was watching a program the other day highlighting the different aspects of the Middle East when I saw all the camaraderie and fellowship that went on and how nice everyone seemed to be while living within the Muslim community among those of like mind. It was then that I realized what has been written portrays Islam, and the Muslims who follow Islam, in a light that might be disturbing to some. It was also then that I realized it isn't the people as much as it is the ideology of the people, or perhaps I should say, it isn't the people as much as it is the faith in a non-Christian religion embraced by the people. Hank Hanegraaff[2] verified this information while on a trip to Iran many years ago.

Hank concludes his discussion of the Iranian people by adding a paradox that seems to exist between Muslims and their religion. He says, "My encounters emphasize the distinction between the Muslim people and the religion they follow. Many Muslims are peaceful and tolerant; however, the history of Islam demonstrates conclusively that it is not a peaceful and tolerant religion."[3] Thus, the paradox.

Inside Islam—Islamic Heritage

To understand Islam, it might help to define the beginning of the thread of the Arabs who eventually became Muslims. And upon becoming Muslims they have a destiny that requires them to

[2] Hanegraaff, Hank. *Christianity in Crisis*. Christian Research Institute Publisher: Rancho Santa Margarita California, 1993.

[3] Hanegraaff, Hank. *Muslim*. West Publishing Group. Nashville, Tenn. 2017.

promote a religion known as Islam. A religion with a destiny that requires the obedience to a set of rules and a very distinct lifestyle. For those outside of the parameters of Islam known as "infidels," well, they are not of much use. Somewhat like cattle that need to be slaughtered. I believe everyone on this planet knows your either with them or you are against them. There is no middle ground.

As we know the relationship between Muhammad, Allah, and the Puppet Master was responsible for bringing forth a fabricated religion, but the seed of that fabricated religion started somewhere, and many believe it was a religion introduced to them by the "angel of light." That might be something worthy of exploring, but first, let us trace some history regarding the heritage of Islam. In retrospect everything seems to begin with Noah and his family.

In the beginning was God as explained to us by way of the Christian Bible. A book that is accepted by Christians everywhere. A book written well before Muhammad and the Qur'an came upon the scene. And in that book the world is told the story of Christianity and the story of eternal life. In that book are many players who assumed different roles in bringing forth the Christianity we embrace today. And in that book, we are told of a tremendous flood that eliminated all the inhabitants of the earth except for eight—Noah his wife and their three sons Ham, Shem, and Japheth, and their wives. Considering this, one can only surmise the world was repopulated by them.

If that is true as most Christians believe, then it would only be logical to assume that from these three sons came the threads that led to the birth of both Christ and Muhammad and established the religious foundation that went with each. From Ham came the religion of Islam and from Shem came the continuation of the thread of Christianity that began with Seth. (Adam and Eve's kid). Then there was Japheth who rounded out the three sons of Noah, it seems he was there just to support Ham.

While Noah's kids went in different directions, two remained cohesive enough to begin building a tower towards heaven, referred to as the Tower of Babel. That is when God scattered the people giving each their own language. This event occurred approximately four generations removed from Noah in the land of Shiner. One thing I realized and mentioned a moment ago, is the linage that led to Muhammad and the Muslim heritage. A linage that began with Noah's kids going forward from the flood. And of the three, it was only Shem that was chosen to carry on the thread of redemption to Jesus, while Ham and Japheth carried on the thread to Muhammad.

It was the descendants of Ham and Japheth that built the tower of Babel. An event from which the city of Babylon came into existence. Babylon, a city with the reputation as a cradle of idols, harlots, or as the Bible says, "She has become a home for demons and a haunt for every evil spirit." Many believe Babylon was a coded substitute for Rome, the city that set on seven hills. Some are even considering the biblical Babylon to be America, but it appears to be Rome that is built on seven hills. It appears in some circles America is considered the Great Satan, but most would probably put their money on it being Rome rather than America.

As the descendants of Noah's kids were spreading across the Middle East and beyond, some of them stood out among the many. For example, Nimrod, the grandson of Ham and the great grandson of Noah. In the land of wondering nomads, various gods, various idols; a land of tribal villages, Nimrod rose to be a great builder. Cities such as Nineveh and Babylon were probably his greatest accomplishments. Also, Micah 5:6, references Assyria as being called the land of Nimrod, and we know how much trouble Assyria brought to Israel. It seemed that every time Israel got out of line, God used Assyria to remind them of their destiny. Most would consider Nimrod perhaps the greatest builder and developer of his time.

Over time and through evolution of procreating, Noah's kids eventually settling over the earth. It is from the loins of Noah that much history has been made for us to witness and some of

4

that history is watching the progression of heirs and how some of them turned out. But the sliver of history that made an everlasting impact upon humanity was brought about by following the linage of Ham and Shem. Mainly Ham, as it was his linage from which Islam and the Islamic god seemed to have evolved.

Why do most consider it to be Ham as the one leading to Muhammad and the introduction of Allah and Islam as opposed to one of the other brothers? Good question. We know it was not Shem as God used him to continue the thread of redemption, just as He did with Seth. That would leave Ham and Japheth, and as mentioned, Japheth was there in a passive role, but in answering the question as to why many think it was Ham's descendants, most would answer by saying; it was because of a curse that was placed upon him. (Genesis 9:22). Of the three boys, Ham was the only one to receive a curse, "The Curse of Ham" as it has been referred to.

This curse came about when Ham saw the nakedness of his father Noah while his father slept. He told his two brothers who were outside, probably in descriptive terms, how he saw his father's nakedness. Noah, upon hearing of the incident, placed a curse upon Ham that has followed his descendants until the calling of Muhammad and the introduction of Allah to break that curse. Ham's descendants, like Adam's son Cain, who was cursed by God, become wondering nomads. Fragmented tribes of wondering Arab's who eventually evolved from the descendants of Ishmael and Esau and were known for visiting cities and bartering merchandise, (It was a band of Ishmaelites that bought Joseph from his brothers and took him to Egypt and sold him to Potiphar[4]).

Karen Armstrong tells us in her book *A History of God* that the wondering bands of nomads felt inferior with low self-esteem

---

[4] Potiphar, also known as Aziz in Islam, is a figure in the Hebrew Bible and the Qur'an. He was the captain of Pharaoh's guard who is said to have purchased Joseph as a slave and impressed by his intelligence, makes him the master of his household.

(I added that one) when they encountered those who always acted loftier to them. Always appearing to be superior and having something they did not have. We can accept it now as having the Spirit of God, the real God, the God of the Jews and Christians, a God ceremoniously embraced by the Jews, and worshiped by the Christians. A God that must have seemed alien to the future Arab Muslims.

Karen tells us that prior to Muhammad and his visitation by the angel Gabriel (more on this shortly), a feeling of inferiority came upon the Arabs when they met Jews and Christians. They were taunted and made to feel inferior for being a barbarous, paganistic group of people. Unlike the descendants of Shem, the future Muslims did not appear to have any revelation knowledge from God. The Jews had the Torah, and Christians, (in this vernacular, I am defining a "Christian" as a follower of Jesus), well, they had a lot of information that appeared to give them wisdom.

Wisdom that seemed to be missing among the nomadic tribes and that seemed to place them in the category of barbarians. The Arabs, who eventually became Muslims, felt a mingled resentment while at the same time feeling respect for those who seemed to have knowledge that they themselves did not possess. It was going to be the wisdom and knowledge from Allah as given to them by Muhammad that was going to change the entire landscape of the Middle East and eventually spread throughout the world.

While the future Muslims had many gods passed down for generations, apparently something was missing. It took Muhammad to give them what they wanted, a God of their own, a God they could believe in and rally around. A God who promised them the world in exchange for obedience. Upon leaving their gods and idols behind and accepting this "one God concept," and accepting as a fact the one bringing it to them to be a prophet, they became followers of an imaginary god. And being a follower of this god, well that comes with a promise—all who follow Allah will one day rule the world. After all, Islam is a religion of dominance.

II

The Conception of Islam

IT ONLY TOOK THE RIGHT formula for the conception of a fabricated god to become a reality. And when that "perfect storm" evolved, that combination allowed for a person known as Muhammad to change the world of religion forever. He accomplished that by introducing a god that would give the future Muslims what they wanted and brought to them by a professing prophet. And, as we know, the world has not been the same since. Who was this guy and how was he chosen? And was he possessed as some contend?

We can probably answer that question but perhaps Charles Kimball[5] describes Muhammad's background as well as anyone. He begins by saying: According to the Quran, Muhammad was the last or "seal" of the prophets charged with conveying God's revelation to humankind. Born in Mecca on April 22, 570 C.E., Muhammad was orphaned at age six when his mother died. His father died before Muhammad's birth, so he was raised by his uncle, Abu Talib. Muhammad was spiritually oriented and known to be an honest, sincere person from an early age. His nickname was *al-amin* ("the trustworthy one").

While on a spiritual retreat at the age of forty, he was confronted by the angel Gabriel, who told him to "recite" what God would reveal to him. That was the beginning of his twenty-two-year prophetic ministry. A ministry that would eventually make him a prophet and introduce Allah into the world. Muslims

---

[5] Charles Kimball. When Religion Becomes Evil—Five Warning Signs. HarperCollins Publisher: N.Y. 2008.)

contend Muhammad to be the last of the prophets. There was Jesus and then Muhammad. It was during the visitation by the angel Gabriel that Muhammad was presented with the knowledge that led to the introduction of Allah and the creation of Islam.

By Muhammad's acceptance of this revelation of *"enlightenment,"* as presented by Gabriel, a religion of deception was unleashed upon the world. A religion designed to deceive the multitudes, or as many as possible, just as it does now, and continues to do so, even as we speak. Is that not what Satan wants? Satan wants nothing more than to eliminate all non-Muslims who will not accept Allah as the rightful god. A god who, according to Muslims, is destined to sit on the throne of David in Jerusalem in place of Christ. So, I ask, is it hard to see Satan's involvement in this whole situation?

If that be true with Islam, perhaps it is true with the unbelievers as well. Can one not see the direction the world is headed? Either Islam or the unbelievers—the radicals of liberalism, those who currently outnumber Christians, those who have an agenda. I'm betting one of those agendas will be to wave goodbye to Christians when we are Raptured. Think about that. We are told, they blame Christians for all the tribulation that is being poured out upon them. Because of this, our departure will succeed in accomplishing, fulfilling their agenda. We are told that they will be so happy, they will even exchange gifts. The Spirit of Christmas seems to exist.

We're talking about an agenda, an itinerary, that God put into motion in the Garden of Eden. And that agenda seems to put Christians in dire straits in the coming future. Either way, Muslims, or unbelievers—the Secularist, Humanist, and New Agers—you know the atheist who make life changing decisions. Those who will continue the act of removing God and His followers. It is just that the unbelievers believe in an "atheist" God; the god of greed, the god of corruption, the god of materialism, and Islam believes in Allah as their god. And the question asked by many is "where did Allah, the god of Islam, come from?" How was he introduced into the world? Or one might even use the words, "the time when he was unleashed upon the world."

The Night of Power

In AD 610, when Muhammad was forty, he had a visitation that would come to be known as the Night of Power. According to Islam, this beginning revelation came to Muhammad in the form of "a gracious and mighty messenger." It was during this visit that the first version of the Quran was revealed to the future Islamic Prophet. Now what was conveyed during this night vision is important information as that was a very pivotal moment in the history of the world.

It was at that precise moment, the moment he had a visitation by a "gracious and mighty messenger," or as many might say, the "angel of light," that the religion of Islam was born—conceived and born. We can question the validity of Islam all day long, but when millions believe in it, then the actions from this belief becomes reality. Many might say dogmatic reality, but reality, nevertheless.

The "angel of light," as mentioned, was the one who introduced Muhammad to a new god, a different god than the one portrayed in the Bible. A god who was the brainchild of Muhammad given to him by a spiritual entity. Based upon that information one might wonder just who, or what was the spiritual entity that visited Muhammad that night? Muslims say it was the angel Gabriel, but most Christians believe it to be the "angel of light" who appeared in the form of the mighty angel Gabriel. The reason Christians don't accept Gabriel as the spiritual entity is the fact that the message delivered to Muhammad was diabolically opposed to the Bible and the teachings Christians follow.

We are all aware of the one who introduced the world to Islam and who initiated a religion of deception that would lead billions of Muslims to a god of their own creation, and that would be Muhammad. Since we already knew that, another question might be, "who introduced Islam to Muhammad?" We just read that it was the "angel of light" that introduced Allah into the world via Muhammad, but just who is the "angel of light?" That we are about to find out as the Bible provides that answer.

The Angel of Light

The "angel of light" is how the Bible explains the one who introduced the deception that exists within Islam. Now the question becomes, who or what is the "angel of light?" For that answer let us turn to Hal Lindsey, one of the foremost futurist preachers of our time. He wrote *The Late Great Planet Earth*.[6] A book that remains among the number one best-selling Christian books of all time. Hal is considered an end time (futuristic) preacher who has been a constant contributor of latter-day prophesy for several decades.

According to Hal—and speaking from a Christian's viewpoint— "there are only two sources of the supernatural: The God of the Bible [followed by Christians] and the god of this world [followed by Muslims and unbelievers] who is described as an 'angel of light'" (2 Corinthians 11:14). It was the "angel of light" disguised as the angel Gabriel, who visited Muhammad that eventful night so that a new revelation leading to a new religion leading to a new god could be introduce into the world.

Just an interesting fact. Muhammad was not the first to be visited by the "angel of light." Remember when Jesus was in the wilderness for forty days and forty nights? He was tempted by the

[6] Hal Lindsey & C.C. Carlson. *The Late Great Planet Earth*. Zondervan House Publishers. Grand Rapids Mich.

same "spiritual entity" as Muhammad. And just like Muhammad, He was promised the world. As we know, He refused to turn from the Creator of the universe, the true God, and bow before the "angel of light."

Twenty years of American sacrifice, thousands of lives lost, and trillions of dollars wasted, for what? So that former President Bush could use the phrase "Shock and Awe" followed by "Mission Accomplished?" But in his defense, many believe he was fulfilling prophesy. The Bible refers to a King of the South and many equate that title with Iran. Prior to Shock and Awe, and with Afghanistan in play, they kept Iran in check. But now, with our withdrawal from Afghanistan, Iran is, once again, quickly becoming America's number one threat—or I should say, "Islam" is becoming our number one threat. And get this, Berkeley students are raising money to send to the Taliban, our enemy. When did America lose its intelligence? But then, they are only the product of what they have been taught.

And what they have been taught has been found to be unacceptable to many Americans, including how Islam has managed a foothold into most of our very schools, our Judeo-Christian schools. Yeah. Right. Judeo-Christian schools. That ship sailed many years ago. Whatever happened to a Judeo-Christian America? if we listen to the latest gallop poll, we find an answer. And the answer appears to be that ship has also sailed, as the poll shows Christians in America numbering less than 50%. Another statistic that might surprise you is the one that says approximately two-thirds of Collage students denounce the authenticity of the Bible as well as Christianity in general. How sad is that? But Christ said it would be this way.

Why would the Creator God be the one to give Muhammad instructions that brought about the Islamic religion causing the situation within the world that currently exists? He didn't. But he arranged for it to happen, and he allowed it to take place. Why? Why would God arrange for another deity who is diabolically opposed to Him to enter the picture? Well, the answer to that question is found in the Garden of Eden as recorded in the Christian Bible.

But to give a short answer would be to say everything has been orchestrated by God and it reads like a story from beginning to end. And that end comes exactly as is described in the books of Daniel and Revelation and confirmed in Matthew Chapter 24. What most, if not all Christians are trying to do now is figure out the players. We know there are spirits who are opposed to Christ roaming the earth, and some ask if it was not one of these spirits who indwelled Muhammad. Some seem to think so.

Was Muhammad Possessed

Based upon the information just presented, it appears to be the "angel of light" portrayed as the angel Gabriel who Muslims declare to be the Spirit of God. And it was this spirit who visited Muhammad and introduced Allah into the world, but some question that claim. Hank Hanegraaff says "he most certainly was not the angel Gabriel (Jibril)."[7] But then common sense tells us the same thing. In the beginning Muhammad thought he was possessed. He spent years trying to convince himself, as well as others, he was not.

It took a great deal of persuasion by his first wife Khadija to convince Muhammad that his encounter may have been divine as opposed to demonic in origin.[8] It was Khadija who was very instrumental in the "birth of a Prophet" becoming a reality. A reality that was instrumental in bringing the heart of the brotherhood of the Arab community to beat as one when they began serving Allah. A heart, from fragmented groups of people, tribes, nomads, and so on, who evolved into a cohesive

---

[7] Hank Hanegraaff. *Muslim*. West Publishing Group. Nashville, Tenn. 2017.
[8] Ibid

unit. As mentioned earlier, the reason to believe the spirit that visited Muhammad that night was evil is the diabolical nature of Islam as opposed to the nature of the real God.[9]

Islam was birthed by a night vision given to an individual by the "angel of light" as opposed to a virgin birth and all the history that preceded that event as well as the history that followed leading to the Crucifixion, resurrection, and salvation. On the other hand, Muhammad is still buried, while Jesus awaits Christians to lavishly reward them with gifts and eternal life. That seems like a no brainer to me. And everyone will be without excuse as Jesus said the Holy Spirit would be given to anyone who asks so they may know the truth and—be without excuse. That also applies to the Secularist, Humanist, and New Agers. Those who seem to be leading the world ever closer to the times as described in the Bible.

Was Muhammad possessed? The answer to the question of Muhammad being possessed with an evil spirit or not, would depend upon whom one asks. Just like the spirits of immorality, depravity, iniquity, and corruption currently can be seen and yet, many seem to be blind. While others seem to be lost for an understanding as to why. It appears the world is continuing down a road that most find very troublesome and ask if there is anyone who can stop the momentum? A question that appears to be on the minds of many, and fortunately, we have a couple of options available.

The Bible leads one to believe it will be the coming of Christ while the Quran tells us it will be the coming of the Islamic Messiah—al Mahdi, who will eventually stop the madness. But in the meantime, the spirit of evil, as brought to us by the "angel of light," and defined by the book of Revelation, seems to be among us. Spirits that seem to be engulfing us and bringing strife and frustration into our life as they remove peace from the world.

---

[9] Ibid

13

A world that many are approaching with a degree of hesitancy, mistrust, and lots of questions. But we were discussing Islam. Prior to Islam's domination of the Middle East, a religion reigned known as Zoroastrianism, but when Islam came calling, this religion went almost extinct. It appears the Middle East has been at war with the Holy Spirit for perhaps, well forever. And we are about to discuss some of that history, including visiting the Holy Kaaba, the home of Allah. But that was not always the situation.

III

Pre Islam—Zoroastrianism

FOR THE FIRST FEW CENTURIES of religious history many factions were emerging, and in so doing they were forming their own opinions of God. The Jews had a God, the pagans had many gods, and Christianity was beginning to emerge as a new way, which left the wondering nomads from the tribes of Ishmael and Esau to produce their own gods. Which is exactly what they did. Before Abraham, as well as after, they brought their gods and idols into the land of Canaan when they settled there.

Thinking about that, one could say they were really dedicated to worshiping idols. Remember Nimrod, Noah's great grandson, a descendant of Ham, and how he was an idol worshiper to the core? As mentioned, it was Ham and Japheth's descendants that were settled in Canaan when God sent Joshua and Caleb to remove them from the promised land and occupy it as their own.

The descendants of Ham and Japheth, from Abraham going forward, became known as Ishmaelites, descendants of Ishmael, and Edomites, descendants of Esau. They were the people who eventually occupied the land of Canaan. They were so deprived they were sacrificing their own children to the many gods they bowed to. As we know, to remove these pagans, God was going to send Joshua and Caleb. But we are only discussing a small portion of the Middle East.

Before Muhammad much of the Middle East consisted of a form of religion called Zoroastrianism from around 600 BC to around 650 AD. *Zoroastrianism!* A monotheistic pre-Islamic religion of ancient Persia, which as we know is now Iran.

Zoroastrianism followers accepted a monotheistic way of beliefs in a polytheistic period, and many applaud that as good, however, the Zoroastrians exalted a deity of wisdom, *Ahura Mazda* (Wise Lord), as its Supreme Spiritual entity. Thus, wisdom became their base of religion more than a superior God.

From this wisdom came some major features of Zoroastrianism that survived time, such as messianism—the advent of a messiah; judgment after death, heaven and hell, and freewill ideas, all of which have influenced other religious systems including Gnosticism, Christianity, and Islam. Zoroastrianism was a religion that served as the state religion of the pre-Islamic Iranian empire for more than a millennium until it lost its clout around the seventh century following the Muslim conquest by Muhammad and his followers of Persia during A.D. 633-654.

Upon this conquest, Muhammad denounced the worshiping of idols, along with any religious entity other than worship of Allah. That was a hard concept to sell in a world full of gods and idols. It was in Mecca, his hometown, that when he tried to convince his brethren of the one God concept, his world clashed with the thinking of the citizens of Mecca, as well as with the roaming nomadic visitors who came every year to worship their god(s) who resided in Mecca. Gods that had been passed down from generation to generation, probably commencing with Ham, but for sure from Nimrod. And the spirit of these gods all resided in the city of Mecca in what has become known as the Kaaba.

The Kaaba of many gods

The Kaaba is a small shrine located in the center of the Great Mosque in Mecca, a sacred shrine in the heart of Saudi Arabia. And is home to a very sacred holy relic referred to as the "Stone from Heaven." An actual stone from the sky that Muslims claim came from heaven. We're going to discuss this later, but for now the wondering nomads had their idols as well as their "gods" and they were residing in the city of Mecca. It was the gods of these various factions who eventually found their way to the Kaaba. (Also referred to as Ka'ba or Ka'bah).

It has been estimated that as many as 360 idols of the Meccan people, as well as "gods" of the various nomadic tribes resided within the Kaaba in the pre-Islamic period. Prior to Muhammad it was a polytheist sanctuary and was the site of pilgrimage for thousands of people throughout the Arabian Peninsula. It was the calling of Muhammad, maybe even a bit destined, to convert these idol worshipers of the same fathers (Ishmael and Esau) to a "god" that was destined to change their world. But that meant the removal of all the other gods that were being worshipped and were residing in the Kaaba.

Muhammad found that to be a hard sell as that required a complete change of thinking regarding all they had ever known. And when he tried to sell it to the citizens of Mecca, they were not having it. That is why Muhammad had to leave Mecca. He was preaching a one God concept that flew in the face of the other Arab roaming nomads who came to Mecca to worship their gods. The various gods, including Allah, who were occupying the Kaaba.

Moved the following down, following the next paragraph. So, delete the following paragraph after moving it.

Because of his radical ideas of eliminating all the gods that occupied the Kaaba except Allah, he had to flee Mecca for Medina when his life became in danger. But he eventually returned to Mecca when his followers were strong enough and had spilled enough blood to claim Mecca and the Kaaba and to put everything under his control. And, as they say, the rest of the story is history.

After the death of Muhammad, Muslims continued to go to Mecca during the period of Ramadan only now they go to revere Allah. They go to worship and honor only one god, but as we have seen, that was not always the situation. Over time, Muhammad had convinced enough Arabs to follow him, but to follow him meant that each of the many nomadic tribes would have to replace the gods they had been worshiping and accept the one and only god concept that was being promoted by Muhammad. Apparently, as evidenced, they did. Because, as we know, Islam is a monotheistic religion.

Regarding the Kaaba, Muslims claim it was Abraham along with his son Ishmael who were responsible for establishing the settlement which today is the city of Makkah (Mecca). And they together built the sacred place for worship in that city. Although, I am not sure a Christian would accept as a fact, Abraham along with Ishmael, building a Holy replica known as the Ka'ba honoring Islam and the god of Islam. Especially since Abraham was following, and fully committed to the Creator God. Besides, as we know, Abraham and Hagar parted ways at the request of Sarah when Ishmael was very young.

The "Stone from Heaven."

Earlier it was mentioned that a stone, a black stone polished by time has been claimed by Muslims to have fallen from heaven and has become the heart of Islam. This is where it gets interesting. They interpreted this object as a guide, a sign, for Adam and Eve to build an altar. That's right. Adam and Eve from the Garden of Eden. Islamic tradition has it that this stone was given to Adam on his expulsion from paradise to obtain forgiveness for his sins. Legend has it that the stone was originally white but has become black by absorbing the sins of the countless thousands of pilgrims who journey to Mecca to pray to Allah as they circle the Kaaba for the required seven times during which they try to kiss and touch the sacred stone. This was a tradition that was established even prior to Muhammad.

It appears that an alter was established in the pre-Islamic period and was a site of pilgrimage of the Nabataeans (ancient Arab people who inhabited northern Arabia and southern Levant) who visited the shrine once a year to perform their pilgrimage that became known as Ramadan. Eventually this became a practice of other Arabs and the beginning of migrating to the small city of Mecca began. As mentioned, it is said that Adam built an altar designating the exact spot the creator God had chosen for all to come and worship. And the Arabs did come, mostly nomadic Arabs, those we have been discussing. They come from across the Arabian Peninsula to worship the gods that lived in the Kaaba.

Another legend has it that God sent a sign in the form of a meteorite, a solid coal black stone, that the Arabs believed had spiritual as well as mystical powers. It was not long before all Arabs would be revering the spot where the meteorite landed and as mentioned earlier, upon which a shrine, known as the Kaaba, was built by Ishmael and Abraham. That would make the year around 2250 B.C., that the Kaaba was erected to house all the various gods the nomadic tribes were worshiping. It was Muhammad's calling to change the dynamics of the entire Middle East and I believe it easy to say, "he was quite successful." But at what cost?

IV

The Slaughter at Medina

BOTH THE CITIES OF MECCA and Medina are especially important in the life of Islam as Muslims teach that the root of Islam began in Mecca and then became defined in Medina. Mecca because of being the birthplace of Muhammad and the home of the sacred Kaaba, and Medina as it is the burial place of Muhammad and the place much blood was shed. Muslims orient themselves toward the shrine in Mecca during the five daily prayers, they bury their dead facing its meridian, and cherish the ambition of visiting it during a pilgrimage, or hajj, in accord with the command as set forth in the Qur'an.

The story behind Medina is somewhat interesting. Because of Muhammad, cities such as Mecca and Medina, the two most popular and holy sites for Islam, with Jerusalem being the third, began to become important because of the history that was being made in those cities. Most historians accept that Islam originated in Mecca and Medina at the start of the seventh century. Mecca because, as mentioned, Muhammad was born in Mecca and fled to Yathrib (Medina) for safety reasons.

Medina was a small Jewish outpost that had been around for about nineteen hundred years before Muhammad journeyed there in 622. Muslims claim Medina is the burial site of the last Islamic Prophet—I'm going to guess, Muhammad, as well as many of the first-generation Muslims. I found that interesting because I have read that Muhammad ascended into the seventh heaven on his white steed from Jerusalem. The third holy site of Islam and the place where Muslims built the Dome of the Rock.

A mosque that sits directly upon the site where Solomon's temple had been built. Was that an in-your-face-moment or what? But back to Medina. One picks up that a lot of hate entered the religion of Islam when Muhammad and his followers were jeered, heckled, and taunted by the Jews residing at Medina. Jews who followed Moses and lived by the law of the Torah. Oh yeah. Who can't see a problem coming from this a mile away?

Medina Persona

There appears to be a lot of facades connected with Islam, and if one follows that facade they wind up in Medina. And because of this, Medina comes with some interesting history as we will see when we discuss Yathrib. Bloody history, but interesting history, nevertheless. When Islamic Muslims listen to Allah, they find it necessary to obey his instructions in bringing about his goals. (Same with Christians towards God). And the results of obeying his instructions promotes a very brutal religion that courts a very brutal lifestyle. We can begin to understand some of the brutality that emerged from the hate we witness from time to time by digging into the origin of that hate. Hate that manifested itself from the actions that occurred at Yathrib. (Medina).

The actions at Yathrib instilled emotions in Muhammad that led to accepting beheadings as a way of dealing with his enemies. To live Islamic, I guess would be to embrace, even emulate, the persona of Muhammad which would instill the desire to follow his examples. Even if those examples included beheading individuals who disagreed with your beliefs. Or those who will not accept Muhammad as a "messenger" sent from "God." Or, showing disrespect towards Allah. An example of punishment for disrespect to a Muslim, and their religion, might be the burying of a woman by her husband and their two children—alive, for reading the Bible, as has been reported. Or burning children to death in front of their fathers.

When Muslims talk about Islam being a peaceful religion, many must ask, is it as peaceful as they say? To answer that question, we look no further than Daniel Pearl and the time when Islamic Muslims were dragging bodies of bloodied and beaten American soldiers to their deaths through the streets for all to witness, and the most disgusting part—for all to spit on. Hey Berkeley, are you listening!

And Berkeley, how does one justify slashing the throat of a human being until it was completely sliced from his head as they did to Daniel Pearl? After which they held it aloft in front of a video camera while the other executioners repeatedly stabbed his bloody lifeless body with the detached head lying on a pile of newspapers just to make the statement: "If our demands are not met, there will be more like this." And there were as we recently witnessed by the beheading of several Christians by the Islamic group referred to as ISIS. Much brutality resonates within the Islamic religion, and it seems to stem from those Muslims who can trace their roots to Yathrib.

The Story of Yathrib

Yathrib was a small Jewish settlement Muhammad fled to when he fled from Mecca in June of 622 after learning of a plot to assassinate him. Muhammad, along with his followers secretly left their homes in Mecca to emigrate 200 miles north of Mecca to Yathrib. Just a side note. The apostle Paul ran into this same persecution when he tried to explain the concept of Jesus to a pagan world. A very foreign concept to the pagans who were into idol worship at the time. And just like Muhammad, he was run out of many a town.

In the beginning when Muhammad arrived in Yathrib after being rejected by his hometown people in Mecca, the Jews of Yathrib were willing to accept him and his followers as it appeared, he was trying to learn and follow the Jewish law as laid down by Moses in the Torah. This lasted for a while, but eventual the Jews began mocking, and to a degree, laughing at the stories of the Muslims and their religion.

But the biggest rejection came when Muhammad tried to persuade them that he was a prophet with a declaration of faith that went like this: "There is no God but Allah. And that he (Muhammad) was the last of the true prophets." Accepting this rejects the God of Abraham, Isaac, and Jacob and that is what turned the Jews of Yathrib against him. Declaring that he was the true messenger of God, pretty much ended the relationship the Jews had with the Muslims, and that is where things are today. The hate that was then is still the hate that is now.

Anyway, before everything went south and came to a grinding halt, to find acceptance with the Jews of Yathrib, Muhammad studied Judaism, which included adoption of the more established traditions such as fasting on the Jewish Day of Atonement and acknowledging prayer three times a day instead of the two as was being observed by the Muslims at that time. Probably the biggest concession for Muhammad was to permit the bonding in holy matrimony of Muslims and Jewish women. And finally, he accepted some of the Jewish dietary laws.

It was upon the Muslim "revelation" of Muhammad being a prophet introducing a new god that he was branded a "false prophet" by the Jews who turned their back upon him and his followers along with their ideology. Thinking back for a moment, I bet it was his one God concept that opened the doors for him and his followers at Yathrib, but when he began to explain his interpretation of just who that one God was, they began to laugh and probably make fun of him and his followers. This mocking and jeering led Muhammad to take justice into his own hands and retaliate against this small Jewish community by a purging (beheading) of the Jews for not accepting his ideas. Upon this victory he built the first mosque and formed an Islamic community in Yathrib—some to be changed to Medina.

Based upon the rejection Muhammad was experiencing from those whom he had considered his own people, not only once but twice, it would probably be logical to assume that a certain degree of hatred toward the citizens of Yathrib as well as Mecca, entered him and his followers at Yathrib. The kind of rejection that allowed hatred to flow through the veins of all who followed Muhammad.

According to Karen Armstrong in her book *A History of God*, Muhammad's rejection by the Jews was probably the greatest disappointment in his life. Hal Lindsey in his book *Everlasting Hatred: The Roots of Jihad* explains what eventually became, not only Muhammad's creed of conduct, but the legacy all Muslims seem to adhere to as he writes:

> This [rejection] infuriated Muhammad. He turned to what would become his standard pattern—the sword. He marched against this Jewish tribe and besieged their village. When they surrendered and came out one by one, they were beheaded. The pattern of "confess Islam or face the sword" was established.

As with yesteryears, today remains the same. It appears the choice the Jews have for survival, as well as the rest of the world, is to confess Islam and bow to their god. That is the only way to be spared an eventual death sentence. Because of the seed of hate that was planted at Medina, we know to live Islamic is to listen to the preaching emphasizing death to Jews and infidels. Living Islam is to accept that as gospel. That creed seemed to be instilled at Yathrib and the creed established was anything but merciful, as we are about to discuss.

A question that some might ask could be, is the God of Christians responsible for such horrendous acts perpetrated upon humanity such as 9/11? That would have to be a no. Or would it be God allowing such atrocities to occur? Let us assume that question to be rhetorical as I'm not sure anyone has an answer. Although, if given a choice between yes and no, I believe many would choice yes.

Muhammad's earliest biographer, Ibn Ishaq, is illustrative of the Islamic sources that chronicle the killings of hundreds of Jews at Yathrib. Jews who were forced to kneel in trenches filled with bodies and blood before being brutally beheaded by Muhammad. This is the degree of punishment he inflected upon a small Jewish community. A community that took him and his followers in and broke bread with them.

> People who were not hurting anyone, but being true to form, Muhammad, for this rejection of not accepting him and his god, killed them— men, women, children, babies, all of them. Don't think that mindset doesn't exist today. Hank Hanegraaff tells us in his book *Muslim*,[10] "The apostle (Muhammad) went to the market of Medina and dug trenches in it. Then he sent for them and struck off their heads in those trenches as they were brought out to him in batches."

Somewhere in the world much plotting in many a mosque regarding our demise is taking place, even as we speak. Plotting to continue the advancement of Islam at any cost, and to remember the time Muhammad spent with the unbelievers of Yathrib and Mecca, and what Muhammad did to rectify the situation. The same Islam that revealed itself at Yathrib is the same Islam that beheaded Daniel Pearl and burned to death children in front of

---

[10] Hanegraaff, Hank. *Muslim*. West Publishing Group. Nashville, Tenn. 2017.

their fathers. The same Islam that shoots women for not being fully attired or gouging out eyes of women for disobeying a man or pouring acid on young schoolgirls for trying to learn something.

These are Muslims our government is embracing by welcoming them into our country—without knowing who they are. But we can't ask that they be vetted, just a sensible thing to do, as that would be considered discriminating against them and seen as an act of racism. All that must be asked is, "Do you serve Allah?" If the answer is yes, then we are inviting an alien god who has vowed to destroy us into our country, and Jesus will be accompanying that god. That's right, that is what they say. Islam believes that Jesus was a real person, even a prophet, and a Muslim. That's right a Muslim. An Arab Muslim who will be aiding al Mahdi in his earthly reign by cleansing the world of all non-believers.

Jesus, Allah's right-hand man

From almost any book one buys to learn about Islam they will learn about Islam. Probably much more than they would like to know, but they will learn. Many books tell of the coming conflicts and disruptions by Islam; many from a secularist view. Still others approach Islam from a Christian standpoint, and in all the writing one constant remains, and that is the coming of the Islamic Messiah. The most anticipated and central sign that Muslims await is the coming of a spiritual leader known as "al Mahdi."

In Arabic "*al Mahdi*" means "the Guided One." He is also sometimes referred to by Shiite Muslims, which would include Iran, Iraq, Qatar, Kuwait, UAE, and several others, as *Sahib Al Zaman* which translated means "the Lord of the Age" and "the Awaited Savior." The coming of the Mahdi is the central crowning fulfillment of all Islamic end time narratives.[11]

---

[11] Joel Richardson. *The Islamic Antichrist* published by WND books.

Muhammad Hisham Kabbani, the founder and chairman of the American Supreme Council of Islam in America (in other words, the head man representing Islam in America) recently reiterated what has been brought to our attention many times regarding the Islamic Messiah. He said:

> We see that the Mahdi [The twelfth Imam from the lineage of Muhammad] will lead a world revelation that will institute a New World Order based on the Religion of Islam. Mahdi will govern the people and establish Islam on earth and Islam will be victorious over all other religions. The Mahdi will offer the religion of Islam to the Jews and Christians. If they accept it, they will be spared. Otherwise, they will be killed, and our prophet Jesus will be Executioner under our Messiah Mahdi.[12]

Wow! Did he just say, "Otherwise they (meaning us) will be killed by our prophet Jesus?" And did he also just say that the Christian Lord and Savior would be working for the Islamic Messiah Mahdi? Another Wow! Then we have Jay Sekulow who gives us our third 'Wow' as he says, "Shiites further believe that Jesus will also return and assist the Mahdi to convert the world to Shiite Islam." And, as mentioned, execute those who will not bow to Allah.

A question asked earlier was, "would one consider it okay to believe that Christ is not the Son of God, but only a prophet who has now become a Muslim and works for the Islamic messiah al Mahdi?" Of course not. Christians know it wouldn't be okay, but that is what Islam preaches through much of their literature. Many, including the pope, are asking Christians to extend an olive branch to the Islamic community in hopes of finding peace.

---

[12] Ibid.

Fair enough, but what happens when they respond by lobbing off people's head? And some of those heads happen to be Catholic as well as Protestant. And I believe it safe to say, many Islamophobics find this removing of heads, troublesome.

According to Islamic literature Jesus is now in heaven with Allah where he awaits to be sent back to earth. They say, "when Jesus shows up, he will be able to correct all the Christians who misunderstood who he was" as they have missed the true message of Allah, and it will be Jesus who sets the record straight.

As mentioned once before, when that time comes, al Mahdi will offer the religion of Islam to the Jews and Christians as well as everyone else. If they accept it, they will be spared. Also, as we know, if they reject Islam they will be killed and "our prophet Jesus will be executioner under our messiah, Mahdi." So says Muslims as conveyed to us by Hank Hanegraaff.

Wow! It appears only a conversion to Islam will suffice, otherwise Jesus will kill us in the name of Allah. Hank concludes in his book *Muslim* "The end of the matter is this. We have laid the straight stick of essential Christian DOCTRINE next to the Islamic counterfeit and by contrast have observed its crookedness. The deity of Christ is denied as he is rendered in Islam a mere 'slave of Allah.'"

A mere slave of Allah. There is so much wrong with what was just said regarding Jesus, as with you, I don't even know where to begin. The group leading the charge to welcome the Islamic Messiah and Jesus as his right-hand man is the reigning power of Iran—Ayatollah Khomeini, backed by the Islamic Revolutionary Guard, along with the former president, Ahmadinejad. All of whom, feel their government (all Shiites) has a destiny to fulfill, and always will, which is to clear the way for al Mahdi ushering in the era of the twelfth Iman.[13] (Iman and Imam are interchangeable).

---

[13] Iman in Islamic theology denotes a believer's faith in the metaphysical aspects of Islam. Its most simple definition is the belief in the six articles of faith, known as arkan al-Iman.

The other eleven Iman's were killed by Sunni's. Another reason for so much animosity to exist between Sunni's and Shiite's. (Saudi Arabia, 90% Sunni) and (Iran, 90% Shiite).

In the Middle East those of Arab origin who chose to follow Christ believing he is the Son of God are referred to as Coptic Christians. Mostly they can be found in Saudi Araba and other Sunni occupied countries. When we hear of a church being destroyed and people killed, it is usually Shiite's blowing up Coptic Christians, Arab Muslims who have accepted Jesus.

Many of the killings coming from churches being blown up by ISIS, and other factions of Islam, are being carried out by Muslims to eliminate all Christians, including the Coptic Christians who have as much right to life in the Middle East as anyone. As Muslims proclaim, it is their destiny to remove all non-Muslims including Coptic Christians from the Middle East, one way or another, dead or alive, doesn't matter, for in the end, Muslims say they will be successful in cleansing the Holy Land of infidel blood.

And when some of that "ethnic cleansing" is discussed along with a discussion of the Islamic Messiah al Mahdi coming to rule the world, rather than a belief in the Christian Messiah, as has been pointed out by Joel Richardson and other concerned citizens, they are branded as Islamophobic individuals who love to spread hate. Haters, haters, who go against the principle of "live and let live." No, not at all. Christians say Islam can worship whatever entity they want, that has no effect upon the Christian community. However, it is a dereliction of responsibility on the part of Islam when they can't discuss what is visibly being played out right before our eyes. And what is visible might cause a major concern for the world and America in particular.

Especially when it comes to the fear of a destroyed America including all who reside there. But then, other countries have that same fear. It is just a matter of time until someone gets paranoid, and when paranoia fuses with insecurity, fear takes over, then you have the makings of a war. Many who speak out against the potential reign of terror Islam can inflect upon the world, including an EMP attack, which causes the world to express concern. Justifiable concern.

And when some of that concern is expressed, including "ethnic cleansing," along with a discussion of the Islamic Messiah al Mahdi, rather than a belief in the Christian Messiah, they are, as pointed out by Joel Richardson, Islamophobic. They are branded as Islamophobic haters. Haters, haters, who go against the principle of "live and let live." No, not at all. Christians say Islam can worship whatever entity they want, as that has no effect upon the Christian community.

Its only when they can't, more like won't, discuss what is visibly being played out before our very eyes that concerns arise. But then we have discussed deception—win at any cost. Many who speak out against the potential reign of terror Islam can inflect upon the world, are branded as haters. And yet, do they realize Islam can destroy America, and nothing is going to deter them from that objective.

Try as we must and being as determined as we are to welcome Muslims into our country, which includes inviting them to dinner, will again, only bring appeasement, and as we have seen that will not work. As has been said, when Islam comes calling, a Muslim will always hear the voice of Allah. And when that voice says to unleash an attack upon America, including an Electro Magnetic Pulse attack, the only question to be answered is, where?

Since several nations could inflect this horrendous atrocity upon us, including Iran, North Korea, Russia, China, Pakistan, and probably some others who hate us and what we stand for, that seems to place a rather huge target on our back. We know an EMP attack is a reality and should be addressed. If Islam continues to do what they have been instructed to do, then one day could lead to an Electro Magnetic Pulse attack.

Some might be asking what exactly is an Electro Magnetic Pulse? It is the possibility of a foreign country exploding a nuclear bomb thirty-five miles above our country, unleashing what is called an electromagnetic pulse (EMP). A bomb that would affect our energy grids with the potential of totally shutting down America for months, if not years. The Islam embraced by Shiite's as in Iran, has this potential and the motivation to accomplish such a dastardly deed, and without any guilt or remorse as they are being obedient to Allah. They realize the panic an EMP attack would cause. This danger continues to escalate as Iran and North Korea make it abundantly clear, they don't trust us and would rather live in a world without us. We hear them say that over and over, as well conveying that message in their literature.

Almost any book one buys to learn about Islam they will learn about Islam. Sometimes perhaps much more than they would like to know, but they will learn. With Islam it comes down to desire. As with Christianity, it is what motivates a person enough to get involved. Many tell of the coming wars, others discuss Islam from a secular viewpoint, while still others approach Islam from a Christians point of view, but in all the books one can read, the one constant that remains, is the coming of the Islamic Messiah to a world that has been prepared for his arrival.

The most anticipated and central sign that Muslims, rather Sunni or Shiite await, is the coming of a man known as "al Mahdi." In Arabic "*al Mahdi*" means "the Guided One." He is also sometimes referred to by Shiite Muslims as *Sahib Al Zaman* which translated means "the Lord of the Age" and "the Awaited Savior." The coming of the Mahdi is the central crowning fulfillment of all Islamic end time narratives.[14] A belief that is probably embraced by Shiite's more than Sunni's. It might be somewhat interesting to discuss the differences between the two factions.

---

[14] Joel Richardson. *The Islamic Antichrist* published by WND books.

V

Sunni & Shiite Differences

WHILE ALL MUSLIMS WHO ACCEPT Islam as a religion bow to Allah and want to eliminate us, they have different motives in mind. Beyond any doubt Muslims, and that is all Muslims who praise Allah, want to eliminate us. After all that is their destiny as given to them by Muhammad, that is the one constancy they all have. They all want to rip our head from our body.

The Shiite's will be promoting a style of Islam that promotes Ahmadinejad's determination, as well as Iran's determination, but more importantly, the determination of the Ayatollah to bring about destruction that is meant to bring forth the Islamic Messiah. Sunni's have a slightly different reason for eliminating us as we will see shortly. As for Shiite's their purpose is to prepare the world for the return of their Messiah al Mahdi. This was recently confirmed for the sceptics as he said on the Islamic Republic Government Broadcast network that:

> "With the reappearance of Imam (al Mahdi) ...conflicts, differences and discriminations that stem from lack of faith and atheism in the society will be eliminated. The shortcomings of religions and schools of thought will be clarified, and Islam will prevail as the perfect pinnacle of faith." Then he continues, "In other words, methods will become one and oneness will appear in people's beliefs."

A melting pot of oneness meaning the world will become of one mind towards Allah. However, to accomplish that feat, the God of the Jews must be eliminated, eradicated, removed, meaning totally purged from history. If the God of the Jews is eradicated, as is Islamic destiny, then Christians are eradicated as well, because of the same God. Our God would be no more. Are you getting the picture?

The next section discusses a group referred to as Wahhabi Sunnis (al Qaeda) who subscribe to a deprived way of life and despise Western culture. Erick Stakelbeck tells us in his book *The Terrorist Next Door* that the Wahhabi's are a sect "highly influenced by Saudi style, as in Saudi Arabia. Wahhabism will be promulgating the ideology of a Sunni sect of Islam"—meaning they will remove us because they don't like us or our way of life. ISIS is associated with this sect of Islam in that they both hate us.

Wahhabi Islam—Sunni

Sunni verses Shiite. It appears that one group will be ushering in the era, or the time of the twelfth Iman (the Islamic Christ), while the other will be promulgating the ideology of a Sunni sect of Islam known as Wahhabism, a sect known for strict adherence to the rule of Islamic purism. (Osama bin Laden was from this linage as is many who hold Saudi passports). As mentioned, Erick Stakelbeck told us in his book *The Terrorist Next Door* that the Wahhabi are a sect "highly influenced by Saudi style, as in Saudi Arabia and ISIS sects. Wahhabism, is a style of living a life replete with all the hatred for Christians and Jews for which that ideology is rightly infamous." After all, we are the great Satan to them with Israel being the little Satan.

ISIS (Sunni) is probably the most recognized terrorist group today, as well as the most brutal when it comes to the mind-set of those who would complete their agenda for Allah. But then, ISIS is so radical it's easy to identify and declare war upon them. Both Iran (Shiite) and Saudi Araba (Sunni—ISIS) have agendas that are detrimental to the world as both groups desire to rule the world.

Sometime back, shortly after 9/11 our presence escalated in Afghanistan and spread into Iraq in 2003 where Americas witnessed what President Bush referred to as "shock and awe." Shortly after that time two American soldiers were murdered in Iraq to "make a statement" about the martyring (according to them) of Zarqawi, the Al-Qaeda operative leader in Iraq. The morning newspaper read: Mutilations: Reports say both soldiers were tortured before they were beheaded. Now get this, Zarqawi was an American citizen who joined al Qaeda and at his demise some Americans declared America wrong for eliminating an American citizen even if he was guilty of planning the demise of Americans. Another one of those "Politically Correct" perplexities.

This is the religion of Islam as followed by those who perpetrate these heinous crimes as instructed by Allah. As recently as 2017, 147 Christians were killed when Islamic Muslims entered a college in Kenya and very methodically went from room to room asking people if they were Christian or Muslim. If they answered Christian, they were shot on the spot. If they said Muslim, they were asked to recite the Muslim creed, and if they couldn't, they were shot as well. Perhaps we need to do the same to them, but that is not the American way which is to welcome them into our country with open arms—the Christian way. Other than those who can't face the truth, everybody else must know that Islam is an enemy of everyone who is not a Muslim.

How about a little more "reality." How do we forget the "burning to ashes" of six children in front of their fathers because someone dared draw a caricature of Muhammad? Think about this. that. You as a parent are beaten as your child is ripped from your arms and tied down just before your child is set on fire, and there is nothing you can do as he is screaming your name. And don't forget the heart that was ripped from the mother of

Daniel Pearl from losing her son in such a brutal manner. That is the Islam many don't want to talk about but that is the reality of Islam. Those are some of the people we have let—invited, into our country with our departure from Afghanistan.

Never a dull moment with Islam as those who follow that religion continue to bring us more "reality" with the constant executions, beheadings, and everything in between. A consistency that is being executed by ISIS and the Taliban along with the dozens of other terrorist organizations. Sometime back the Islamic State terror group, known as ISIS, pushed two gay men, blindfolded, to their deaths from a roof in Homs, Syria. After plummeting to the ground, with their heads splattering on the concrete, they were stoned by an angry mob, which included children. Children! Can you imagine that?[15]

Shortly after that, the U.K. based Observatory for Human Rights estimates at least 25 people have been killed by ISIS for being gay. Six stoned, three shot in the head and 16 thrown from high-rise buildings. While it appears, Islam is no discriminator when it comes to rendering judgment and inflecting pain, there is one constant among them all. And that, as we have seen, is the lack of respect they show gays, and women. But they take brutality of women to an entirely different level. And since they hold babies and small children up as shields to protect themselves when engaged in conflict, it appears they have no heart for them either.

If it's a woman, in most cases they just shoot her if she is doing something the men disapprove of or dislike. That is of course after berating her, raping her, and desecrating her body. Once again, I must ask, is this the God of the Christian Bible? Is this behavior acceptable in America? Of course not, and yet, we welcome Muslims into our country by the thousands, tens of thousands, and go out of our way to make them feel welcome.

---

[15] The Washington Times—Monday, June 13, 2016, by Kelly Riddell.

An example of what I am talking about. Sometime back, several women arranged a baby shower for Syed Farook and his wife, Tashfeen Malik. Something they wish they could do over. More on them in a minute. But for now, a discussion regarding the treatment of Islamic women might be of interest to some. While others may be absolutely disgusted by it. But again, authenticity is revealed to those who are looking at Islam through the mirror of truth, as the reality of Islam is reflected back. The following is a reflection that the world sees regarding Islam and their treatment of women.

VI

The Women of Islam

WHEN IT COMES TO ISLAMIC women they are viewed as second-class citizens legally, socially, and culturally. From where many sit, being a woman who is considered a second-class citizen in Islam might be a step up. And considering that, one must ask why women accept that, the perspective of women considered less than equal—why? Why would women accept that treatment and disrespect? And in addition to that, they are made to feel through guilt, shame, and disrespect to Islam, that it was the woman's fault. Are they that brainwashed?

Only within the last few years, because of pressure brought about by the social structure of the current world, is the attitude towards women slowly changing. Yet, women are still subservient to men in every way. Again, that was witnessed after the Taliban returned to a position of authority in Afghanistan. And don't forget students at Berkeley University in California have been fund raising for the Taliban. How crazy is that?

Within the Islamic community it seems as if there are different rules for men and women that govern the behavior of each. And much of that difference has to do with the way sex is viewed—sex, temptation, and lust. To deal with temptations, Islamic law—Sharia laws governing lust, sex, and temptation-will in most cases, find the woman is to blame, and the price to pay is horrendous. As we are told by Charles Kimball in his book, *When Religion Becomes Evil,* Islamic males may perform "female circumcision," or female genital mutilation instead of shooting or stoning a woman. This painful procedure is done on young, pre-pubescent girls. I'm sorry, but that must be the most disgusting thing any human could do to another. And that is okey with the god they worship and praise and follow. Wow!

The degree of mutilation varies, but it involves scraping away all or part of the clitoris and sometimes the labia. It is estimated that today "one in five Muslim girls lives in a community where some form of clitoridectomy is sanctioned and justified by local Islamic leaders." And Berkeley University students are fund raising for these fine people. In other words, sanctioning what they do. And these kids have parents.

Lust when combined with covetousness is an awful thing to a Christian, and many preachers tell us why. Especially those preachers who follow the "Christianity," if I may, that many define as "followers of Jesus." That narrows it down just a bit. Christianity can mean several things but when one says they are a follower of Jesus that narrows it down just a bit. When it comes to lust within the Islam community, they believe women cannot control their sexual urges, when in fact, it is the men who cannot control there's. I never heard of an Islamic man being stoned to death for being consumed with pornography.

Just thinking out loud. That is also one of the reasons Islamic women wear a Burka or Niqab. Clothing designed to cover their bodies. Of course, they wear the Burka out of respect for their religion and respect for Allah and because they were taught it is the proper clothing to wear to honor the Islamic faith. Although, this might appear to many to be for the control of the men's sexual urges since the women are not free to choose the clothing they desire to wear.

That was obvious on May 7th of this year when the Taliban introduced a new law that makes wearing of the burka compulsory for women in Afghanistan. I'm betting there was not one woman present when that decision was made. The new law follows the shutting of secondary schools for women in Afghanistan. These actions demonstrate that the Taliban's promises to honor women's rights when they seized power in August of 2021 were idle jesters of appeasement. But in the interest of high morals and standards as set by the Taliban, women must curtail their desires and urges by fully clothing their bodies. Therefore, helping to quench the desires of the men.

And when men have those lusty desires, it must be the fault of the woman, therefore, she must be punished or killed for the good of Islam as defined by Sharia Law. Meanwhile, they can brush off the human rights abuses against women and minorities as defending Islam against "all impurities labelling them as cultural stains not consistent with their own enlightened understanding of Islam." What we seem to have here is a "communication problem." What we have discussed so far would qualify for a Stephen King novel, and yet, the brutality within Islam seems to know no boundaries.

Brutality Coming to America

How about a couple more examples illustrating the brutality of a peaceful religion? A religion as we have been witnessing that is coming to America, along with those who support it. To understand the Muslims who will be coming to America, and who will be demanding special treatment, let's turn to Jay Sekulow's book, *Unholy Alliance*[16] and read where he says, every day—every single day, we see horrific headlines from somewhere in the world. It's as if we almost expect them. Now remember this was written prior to Covid becoming headline news and has somewhat distracted us from the threat of Islam. But then, we witnessed the true heart of Islam, upon our departure from Afghanistan:

---

[16] Sekulow, Jay. *Unholy Alliance*. New York, New York. Howard Books Publisher. 2016.

Terrorists burn entire villages to the ground, with the children's wailing heard miles away. Christian men are forced to kneel above explosives that are detonated by jihadists. Crucifixions are not uncommon, beheadings almost become a way of life. Christians are buried alive—men, women and children, missionaries' sons and daughters are slaughtered.

And students at Berkeley University are raising money to send to them. But more sadly, "people are giving money." Perhaps even more sadly is the fact that parents raised these students. The following is a very interesting story passed along to me by a friend that elucidates, reveals, and even exposes the mind-set many Muslims have towards Christianity and the Bible. Recently a case of inhumanity towards everything Christians stand for and the awesomeness of Christ was revealed to us by an Egyptian News agency. (An Egyptian News agency. That is unbelievable.) Anyway, a Muslim man in Egypt killed his wife because he caught her reading the Bible. (There are many "closet Christians" who live in constant fear of Islam.) Then he buried her along with their infant baby and an 8-year-old daughter, who were both buried alive as well.

After 15 days, the girls were accidentally discovered alive by the digging of another grave. According to the 8-year-old, they were kept alive by a man wearing shiny white clothes with bleeding wounds in his hands. The circumstances surrounding the situation, were miraculous to say the least. The 8-year-old said, "Jesus came every day and woke up her mother so her baby sister could nurse." Amazing! Simply amazing. What man saw as evil (reading the Bible) and reacted to as evil, Christ turned into good. A tremendous miracle.

While the above atrocities are being committed, we are told of women who are sold into sex slavery—the younger the girl, the higher the price. This pedophilia is occurring right here in America as well as within the elite of the Catholic church. Radical Islamic terrorist even distribute pamphlets that are read by most, if not all Muslims, explaining how Islamic law does not forbid the rape of young girls. Wow! Again, does that sound like the God of the Christian Bible? I believe most would say no, however, how does one ignore the facts? Facts that describe what happened December 16, 2014, when seven Taliban militants attacked a school in Peshawar, Pakistan, killing at least 145 people, the clear majority of whom were children between the ages of twelve and sixteen.

In justification of such atrocities, the key moderate voices of Islam all agree that Islam, per se, has nothing to do with terrorism. We will discuss shortly where this thinking originated. Now think about what your about to read. Sometimes those who follow Islam are unbelievable as they say, "racism and western foreign policy are the roots of Islamic grievances, and those who disagree with that are fringe conservatives."

Now their labelling many Americans as racist who are grounded in conservative western roots. Roots that include Judeo-Christian thinking. And because of this, we bring grievances to Muslims. Really? It sounds like they are saying the roots of Judeo-Christian thinking bring grievances to them, to Muslims. Bring grievances to them. Our western culture brings grievances to them. And how do they deal with those grievances? They say the root must be removed. And who might be the root? According to them—everyone who is not Muslim, but especially those who serve the Christian God. Again, are you getting the picture?

Yassmin Abdel-Magied (an Islamic activist) once said "For me, Islam is one of the most feminist religions, and that Islamic terrorism is a media creation of such trends that some have been embraced and promoted enthusiastically by cultural and media institutions." In other words, media hype is responsible for the way Islam is viewed. It is embarrassing as those views of Islam being a "media creation" appear to be either denial of, or appeasement of, or repression of the most uncomfortable aspects of Islam. Media hype did not cause 9/11 or the thousands of deaths attributed to Islam.

I am quite sure Yassmin is familiar with the controversial case of an Iranian woman Reyhaneh Jabbari who was hanged in Tehran October of 2014 for the murder of a man she claimed attempted to rape her. Her sentence was supported by the concept of *qisas*, a word found in the Quran. The term *qisas* is translated as "equality in retaliation," meaning that any injury inflicted upon another should be compensated for by punishing the perpetrator with the same injury. An eye for an eye. The justice of *qisas* is used in Islamic law to support men's superiority over women.

VII

R-Rated Brutality

THERE ARE UNDENIABLE DEGREES OF torture. The torture that has been brought to our attention by Erick Stakelbeck and Bill Bennett's book: *The fight of our Lives,* is hard to digest. The type of torture used during the Saddam Hussein era and is consistently being used today throughout the Middle East in the quest to acquire information and loyalty, and for demanding obedience to Islamic law.

Such torture includes (and I would probably give this an R rating) gouging out the eyes of children to force confessions from parents and grandparents. This type of torturer is not hesitant to crushing all the bones in the feet of a two-year-old girl to force her mother to divulge her father's whereabouts, or someone who will hold a nursing baby at arm's length from its mother, allowing the child to starve to death to force the mother's confession to Islam. Now don't forget, according to them, we are discussing a religion that embraces equality and peace. A group that Berkeley students are raising money to send them showing their support. Did I mention that these kids have parents?

Many might remember when Muslim militants in Syria tried to force two Christian women and six Christian men to convert to Islam. Upon their refusal, the women were brutally raped before being beheaded alongside the men. The same day militants cut off the fingertips of a twelve-year-old boy in a failed attempt to force his Christian father to convert. When the father refused the forced conversion, he was tortured and subsequently crucified in front of his son in adherence to the Quranic command: "I will cast terror into the hearts of those who disbelieve." From Hank's book *Muslim*.

These are people who will burn a person's limbs off to force him to confess or comply with the laws of Islam, people who will slowly lower victims into huge vats of acid for confessing homosexuality. People who bury alive their wife and children for reading the Bible. People who throw acid into the face of young girls, disfiguring them for life, for nothing more than the desire to get an education. It goes on and on, but you get the idea. This is the religion of Islam.

All anyone can say about having this information is…Wow! How can anyone deny the possibility that this stuff comes straight from the land of demonic spirits. And by having this information, it allows us to grasp thoroughly the idea that these are not normal people we are dealing with. And one could even make a stronger case for two Gods, two spiritual entities as we will discuss later. One God could not have the mind-set of the above and have been capable of inspiring the writing of the Christian Bible. That would seem to be an implausible act.

We know not all Muslims have the desire to kill someone or to torture them written upon their heart but there are enough (we will discuss how many a bit later) who possess the satanic nature to bring forth agonizing degrees of "Islamic Justice." Justice that appears to many to come directly from the pits of hell. Would the Christian God condone such action? Does the Christian God convey the message of "become a Christian or die," and then provide an army to bring about his demands? Again, how does one ignore the facts of Islamic brutality? And yet many Americans seem to be doing just that. I can already hear the fury from many Muslims who dislike what has been written, but that is a "kill the messenger" mentality, rather than looking at the problem.

What has been revealed about Islam should be enough to convince anyone of the true God and not the fabricated one that was brought to us by Muhammad and introduced into the world by the one who is controlling Islam, the Puppet Master, the "angel of light." And we as Americans are welcoming them into our country, inviting them to dinner, even throwing them baby showers days before they kill those who were nice enough to throw them a baby shower. Islamic brutality was illustrated with the killing of innocent individuals by Syed Farook and his wife, Tashfeen Malik. You remember them.

A Muslim couple who was invited to a baby shower arranged for her by friends she worked with. Friends who were killed by the couple just a few days later. The very people who gave them precious baby things were raised up and killed. Regarding the party arrangers, one might surmise they were kind and generous friends who gave their time thinking of others. A baby shower thrown by friends who the couple later killed, murdered in cold blood, in the name of Allah.

If this was an isolated situation and not the norm then one might consider Islam to be a peaceful religion, especially if Muslims spoke up and denounced such actions, but we hear crickets. Based upon this silence we must turn once again, to saying actions speak louder than words. I'm sure I'm not the only one who believes Islamic terrorist—those bringing about the violence we witness from time to time, the front-line jihadist, would not be stopped dead in their tracks if we had the cooperation of the Muslim community.

Unfortunately for Americans, if the Muslim community serves Allah, they will continue assisting those who spread the Islamic form of ideology even unto their death, all the while denying having any part of the violence. As we are about to find out, they are the "other guys." The ones defined in the Quran as saying, "The blood of the infidels in the Islamic lands may be shed with impunity and that Muslims should slay wherever ye find them."[17]

---

[17] Jay Sekulow's book, *Unholy Alliance*

They are saying stay out of our country or you will be killed. Fair enough, however, Muslims kill anyone, anywhere, and at any time. And that in the minds of many, is a very dangerous situation, and an intimidating situation for those who understand Islam. Those who dare to expose the truth of Islam. There are many who deny the truth without any understanding of what they are denying. And these are people who have a lot of say regarding how we live our life.

Deniers of Truth

Former US attorney general Loretta Lynch underscored Syed's supposition following the terrorist attack in San Bernardino (Sacramento, San Bernardino, one or the other) by reminding everyone Islam is not to blame. Her first public appearance was with a Muslim advocacy group to express what she designated her "greatest fear"—that Muslims and Clergy (Iman's) would unjustly be implicated by the deeply held Islamic convictions of shooters Syed and his wife Tashfeen. She went on to say that Islam does not in any way encourage violence. Really. Many must have missed that class. While I have not heard of any incidences since, that does not diminish from the fact the possibility exists.

Charles Kimball[18] told us earlier, he is not the only one who feels Islam might be a religion of peace. He says high ranking officials such as the former secretary of state John Kerry along with Condoleezza Rice under former president George Bush along with the former Canadian prime minister Tony Blair all emphasized how peaceful of a religion Islam is while defending the Islamic brutality of the religion. I guess we cannot have enough friends, even if they want to kill us.

---

[18] Charles Kimball. When Religion Becomes Evil

In addition to these individuals, many within the Democratic party, mainly, representatives Alexandria Ocasio-Cortez (AOC), Omar Rashida Tlaib, Ayanna Pressley, Ilhan Omar and probably some within the Republican party as well (nothing political just facts) express anger towards anyone who describes Islam as a religion other than peaceful and tolerant. They say the acts of those people, referred to as jihadist, those who perpetrate violence, do not represent Islam. But since violence is applauded by all Muslims, one would have to question the thinking of those who consider Islam a peaceful and tolerant religion.

Former president Obama and his senior personal adviser Valerie Jarrett who herself was a Muslim went further, noting that the United States and Muslims worldwide "share common principles—principles of justice and progress, and tolerance and the dignity of all human beings." Once again from Hank's book *Muslim*. But then many believe that former president Obama and current president Biden are Muslim sympathizers, who, along with many, have, and are continuing to bring America to its knees.

One must ask themselves if our intelligence is being challenged, or if we are really that uninformed? If we are as uninformed as Condoleezza Rice, the Bush's, the Obama's, the Biden's and so on, along with several others, who harbor the same understanding of Islam, then many might say, "we as a nation are doomed." But in defense of Islam, it is the other guy who causes the problems. The uninformed Muslims. Good Muslims are removed from the bad Muslims as only bad Muslims preform such dastardly deeds as 9/11, and the beheading of people, or burying them alive. And again, if it's a woman, they would probably just shoot her. Yeah! But according to Islam, it is the "other" guy.

VIII

The Other Guys

HAVE YOU EVER NOTICED WHEN someone is accused of wrongdoing, if they are guilty, they always reflect? It is always someone else's fault. The same applies with Muslims following Allah. When a killing occurs, it was the other guys, those Muslims who don't understand Islam. That would be somewhat like saying, "yeah, those who perpetrate such heinous crimes are Muslims alright, but they are the 'other guys' the bad Muslims." According to Islam they appear to be Muslims who don't understand the Quran, at least that is according to Charles Kimball.

I guess living Islamic only applies when it's understood. Everything about this conversation defies logic and as many might say, "it insults the intelligence of others." As with you, I don't know how evil can be considered good. And yet, the dastardly deeds of "the other guys," the other Muslims, those radicals, those jihadists who kill while shouting Allahu Akbar Allahu Akbar seem to find a way. We are told by what appears to be the "good guys" that they are Muslims who are misled and are not to be included when judging Islam.

The "other guys," those Muslims who are uninformed, those who do not understand the true intent of Islam, or the Quran. Muslims who would otherwise be incapable of carrying out such dastardly deeds in the name of Allah if they understood Islam. I guess that is what they are saying. That only the "bad guys," were capable of 9/11. And when Charles Kimball says the actions of Islamic extremist is out of the norm of what Islam is all about, somewhat defending radical Islam, he must be talking about "the other guys."

The "good Muslims" wouldn't think of committing such reprehensible deeds. The Muslims who are our neighbor's, those we may even work with, they will always be the good guys until the religion of Islam comes calling. When it does, a Muslim is a Muslim, is a Muslim, and always will be. Since all Muslims follow the instructions of Allah, how can there be bad guys and good guys. Both "good" Muslims and "bad" Muslims attend the same mosque, pray to the same god, read from the same religious book, so how can there be good Muslims and bad Muslims? Is there a "good" Quran and a "bad" Quran? Of course not. It appears ALL Muslims continue to pursue the same goal, and that is to achieve victory for Allah.

So, with this information, I'm not sure what Charles Kimball and the other deniers base their information on when they contend the terror perpetrated by Islam stems from a misunderstanding regarding the concept of Islam. They say that if everyone understood it, they would realize how peaceful it is. Charles believes this or at least he writes those sentiments in his book. Note: Charles wrote probably the most middle of the road book regarding Christians, Jews and Muslims I have ever read. I was very skeptical at first as it was recommended by a Muslim recruiter, (troll) but I'm glad I read it. We don't agree on several things regarding Islam, but it was interesting to read his opinion.

Charles appears to be sympathetic to the quest of Islam and, for the most part, seems to justify the motives behind their actions, while at the same time claiming to be a Christian. I'm going to assume a very *liberal* Christian, but, according to him, a Christian. When Charles thinks peaceful coexistence is possible to obtain, he is thinking along the same lines as those who promote Chrislam, as well as those who follow Secularism and Humanism, as an answer for peace, but many would have to disagree.

Even if both parties could join physically and live side by side, we would be extremely limited in our dialog. This wouldn't mean much to a secularist, but it would to a Christian. There would never be a joining of the minds on whose "religious" ideology is right or which God we accept, and so on. And if the truth be known deep down, I, perhaps as with Juan Williams, would always remember Syed Farook and his wife and what they did to supposed friends.

Christians and Jews could live in peace with Muslims, that has been proven over and over, contrary to what the Muslims in Congress say. Israel has proven they could live in peace, with Muslims, but not with the Islamic religion. Christians say the same thing. Muslims being true to Allah could never find peace living among the Jews, Christians, or infidels. Their words, not mine. Again, to accept anything other than the true intent of Islam is appeasement, and this lull in Islamic terrorism is just that, a moment of peace. Those sleeper cells are still among us just waiting for the word.

That is how "good" Muslims become "the other guys" and that will always happen when Allah comes calling. Again, I believe we could apply that to Syed Farook and his wife Tashfeen Malik. When Islam came calling, they answered by killing good people. That is part of their heritage, their destiny, to kill infidels in the name of Allah and receive rewards at the conclusion of this journey. The more heinous the crime towards infidels, and the more glory they bring to Allah, the better the rewards.

Remember the root, the core, the etymology if you will, is the same in all Muslims as they get their instructions, their inspiration for living, for thinking, for existing, even for the air they breathe, from a different book than do Christians. And that book explains why our demise is necessary. Having said that, maybe we can understand some of the apprehension Juan Williams might have been experiencing when he was boarding that plane. Perhaps there just might have been a bad guy or two aboard. In other words, a couple of—the "other guys."

The Art of Communicating

Considering the determination of Islam, and the word Quraysh (a deceptive mind) exists in the Muslim vocabular, I believe most can understand the desire of Muslims who follow Muhammad to talk peace and harmony leading one to believe we might just be able to work things out and find harmony together.

Then "we" would all be talking about "us" rather than "us" talking about "them" or "them" talking about "us," but remember the word Quraysh, which means to "Negotiate peace with your enemies until you become strong enough to annihilate them" still exist within the Muslim vocabulary. So sometimes "us" talking to "them" accomplishes nothing, as history has proven several times. Islam has been holding back for centuries claiming to be a nonviolent religion while continuing to spread ideology that can only be quenched by complete dominance.

What we are witnessing, and might witness in the future, is oppression of fourteen hundred years boiling to the surface demanding rights that are contrary to a Christians beliefs. If this sounds strange, then look behind the scenes, or better yet, understand what is being said within the covers of this and other books describing the intent of Islam. The Islam we are going to discuss next. Once that is understood, I'm not sure any amount of communication will deter Islam. But we keep trying, even inviting Islamic Muslims to dinner.

Within the book by Charles Kimball, Wilford Cantwell Smith, a monumental figure in Islamic studies and the comparative study of religion, summarized the trends in scholarly circles when he introduced an excellent concept of how to communicate. It went something like this; in our communication with each other, we communicate better when we use "us" "we" and "they" when he wrote the following:

> The traditional form of Western scholarship in the study of other [religious traditions] was that of an impersonal presentation of an "it." The first great innovation in recent times has been the personalization of the faiths observed, so that one finds a discussion of a "they." The next step is a dialogue where "we" talk *to* "you." If there is listening and mutuality, this may become that "we" talk *with* "you." The culmination of the process is when "we all" are talking with each other about "us."

Communication, that's all that is. The ability to communicate makes leaders, saves marriage, and to many, makes Christians. There are those who believe war might be averted because of communication with North Korea, and some other enemies of America—if more time had been spent communicating. But again, this is only appeasement. And many believe we are running out of appeasements. Time will tell. But one thing is certain, there are some who will always be on the side of anyone who attacks the Great Satan. And that applies to those who would destroy America from within as well as from without. That is why it is dangerous to the health of America to vote Muslims into governmental positions. Anyway, Wilford continues:

"We live in a dangerous world in which many people talk of a 'we' and a 'they.' (Sort of like what is being done within the pages of this book). Wilford Continues: "Religion is at the heart of what matters most to the clear majority who inhabit this planet."

While that may be true, a recent Gallop poll had Christians numbering less than 50% in America. And this is in America, the only real bastille of Judeo-Christianity in the world. Think about that for a minute. And with the removal of Christians, who is taking their place? Secularist and Humanist for some, with New Agers mixed into the fray. Scary when one thinks about it. And there is no end in sight that leads one to believe Islam, as well as those who back Islam, will give up any time soon.

American Islamic States

It appears to many that all the results of God's orchestration of end time prophecy to prepare the world for his coming are approaching more rapidly than most expected. Islam and the Muslim society, culture, values, principles, and religion, in other words, Islam in general and Sharia law specifically, as brought to us by the Quran, as brought to us by Muhammad, as brought to us by Allah, as brought to us by the "angel of light," will play their part upon the world stage in preparing the world for the final events that are currently playing out before our very eyes.

For example, Michigan, the state that has elected Muslims to protect and defend our nation were being allowed to swear in using a Quran as was the Solicitor General. Have the people of Michigan lost their minds. The only way to justify this betrayal is to be a Muslim liberal saturated State. There can be no other reason. Islam is coming to divide and conquer, and a foothold has been established as Michigan and Minnesota have proven. Between Islam pursuing our extinction and a government that is redefining America, as well as American values, Christians will soon find themselves becoming an expendable commodity. "What ever happened to America?" Well, for one thing, we are killing our babies while Islam promotes procreation.

Islam is now the third largest religion in the United States, after Christianity and Judaism. In addition to the states mentioned many Muslims are being settled in New Jersey, Texas, Florida, and in 2017, 20 states mostly in South and Midwest reported Islam to be the largest non-Christian religion and growing. And more and more Muslims who follow Islam are finding their voice, even in running America.

America might one day find that In Islam the laws of Islam allow extremist to bring judgment upon the world which in turn justifies the purging and cleansing that takes place from time to time. And this purging and cleansing is usually conducted without any trial or any semblance of jurisprudence. This is more Wahhabism Islam as in Sunni beliefs, as in Saudi Arabia, as in al Qaeda as in Osama bin Laden. Then there is Muslim ideology, as in the beliefs of Shiite's. Belief's, as in Iran and Afghanistan who give us the Talban. Those who want to eradicate everyone to make way for their Messiah, al Mahdi. And some American states are helping them to accomplish this goal.

In addition to being desirous of our demise, all Muslims loyal to Allah _have shown no forbearance, no mercy, no lenience, in the degree of torture they are willing to impose._ If that includes killing all non-Muslims, then so be it. That is demonstrating obedience and loyalty to Allah for which they receive more rewards when they meet him. As mentioned, we will discuss rewards later. But first it might be interesting to provide proof of the true intent of Islam, regardless of what they say. As we have seen, what Muslims who follow Allah say, and what they do, are totally different. Am I not telling the truth?

IX

The Proven Intent of Islam

JOIN, DIE, OR BE OWNED by Islam, not much grey area there. And heaven forbid if someone should do or say anything against Muslims, especially Muhammad, as this will precipitate protests, such as burning our flag, stomping on pictures of our president, and, once again, hearing "Allahu Akbar, Allahu Akbar" ("Allah is great, Allah is great") across the Middle East. Also, as has been witnessed on more than one occasion, disrespect the religion of Islam by burning a copy of the Quran, and upheaval is felt around the world by followers of Islam. Let's call them Merciless Avengers, killers, hit men, and ask the question, just how many Islamic "avengers," the "other guys" are there? That is what we are going to discuss.

But first, if there was ever any question as to the intent—I mean the "true" intent of Islam, let us listen to what an Imam, someone who is educated, someone who knows the very root of Islam, had to say when asked a question by Rick Mathis, a well-known leader in prison ministry. Information I found from his website. By the way, according to Rick, the Muslim religion per capita, is the fastest growing religion in the United States. Just something to think about. And that was said prior to the current influx of thousands of Muslims who began entering our country when we left Afghanistan.

Regarding the information you are about to read, the Islamic community, as well as many who are not of the Islamic faith, came down hard on Rick when he shared a very interesting experience he had recently while attending an annual training session required for maintaining his state prison security clearance. Probably not as hard as they did on Joel Richardson and others, but they let their presence be known. Rick said, he could even feel the disapproval of those present when he began asking questions.

What he brought to light (a light we already knew existed) was material that was informative as well as enlightening. Rick said, "During the training session there was a presentation by three speakers representing the Roman Catholic, Protestant, and Muslim faiths, with each explaining their beliefs." Rick continued, "I was particularly interested in what the Islamic Imam had to say,"

The Imam gave a great presentation of the basics of Islam, complete with a video. After the presentations, time was provided for questions and answers. When it was my turn, I directed my questions to the Imam and asked: 'Please correct me if I'm wrong but I understand that most Imams and clerics of Islam have declared a holy jihad [holy war] against the infidels of the world and that by killing an infidel they are assured a place in heaven. If that's the case, can you give me the definition of an infidel?'"

Great question, which begged the next question, following the Imam's response to the first question which, without hesitation was, "Nonbelievers." Mathis responded with, "So let me make sure I have this straight. All followers of Allah have been commanded to kill everyone who is not of the Islamic faith so they can have a place in heaven. Is that correct?" Great question! Mathis said the expression on his face changed from one of authority and command to that of a little boy who had just been caught with his hands in the cookie jar. Then Mathis said, "He sheepishly replied, 'Yes.'" He "sheepishly" (embarrassedly, guiltily) said, YES. Yes! To what? To ripping our heads from our bodies for not accepting Allah as our only god, and for not accepting Muhammad as a replacement for Jesus. That is exactly what he said. But remember, that is only the "bad guys of Islam." As for the rest, they only root for the "bad guys" all the while supporting them. Again, a deceptive religion.

As mentioned, after this information was published, Mathis come under considerable pressure and criticism for publishing what he perceived as being the truth regarding the true intent of Islam. In other words, Islamic Muslims tell us what they want us to believe, what they want us to hear, and that is to convey the message they are pursuing a path to live in peace and harmony. Anything beyond that is perpetrated by the other guys—bad or misunderstood Muslims. Yet when questioned, studied, and researched, we find what Muslims who follow the instructions passed down through many generations by the Quran actually stand for. And it is anything but peace when it comes to cohabitating. We as Americans want to believe them about Islam being a passive religion, but facts are facts, and facts don't change with words.

Was Mathis politically incorrect when he brought our attention, once again, to the fact that from the mouth of Islam, they want to eliminate us. Listening to Charles Kimball, author of *When Religion Becomes Evil,* (pg. 64) who brings to our attention Islamic "rationalization regarding killings that take out infidels and Jews" one would assume Mathis to be right in what he exposed as intent of Islam and brought to our attention. After reading what Charles has written about the desires of Islam it confirms what Mathis said to be the truth about eliminating us. Charles perhaps even elaborates much more intently when he says:

> These extremists in Lebanon and Palestine[19] justified the attacks on Jews [and infidels] from passages in the Qur'an... "Fight in the cause of God those who fight you, but do not begin hostilities; for God does not love such injustices. [And yet in the very next breath] Kill them wherever you find

---

[19] It was Omar Rashida Tlaib who encouraged President Biden to give the thousands of Palestine's safe passage to America regardless of their religious or political affiliation.

them and drive them out from the places where they drove you out for persecution is worse than slaughter; but fight them not at the sacred mosque, unless they [first] fight you there; but if they fight you, slay them. Such is the reward of infidels." (2:190-91).

This war was brought to America when the first mosque was built in America. Fight them, slay them as that is what they deserve. Just additional conformation. According to them, we are only worthy of death, like cattle to be slaughtered. How can anyone with any degree of intelligence deny that fact after hearing it directly from a very learned Islamic clergy? I know many Americans want to deny facts, but facts are still facts. Was Mathis right in what he heard and conveyed as fact? According to what Charles Kimball just brought to our attention, it sounds as if he was. And that slaughter continues even to this very day somewhere in the world.

According to Steve Hill in his book *Spiritual Avalanche*,[20] the sword of Islam is still very active. Hill tells us that more than sixteen thousand baskets are filled every year with heads of Christians lobbed off with a four-dollar machete. Wow! That is a big number. Another big number is the estimated 90,000 last year who were killed for their faith, according to the May 3, 2017, edition of "*The Lutheran Witness*." And, according to them, it continues.

Did that get your attention? It certainly got mine. I found those numbers somewhat staggering. And many believe this is only going to intensify as we head into the future, especially now that we have given Islam a foothold in America. But more importantly in the world. I am thinking of Europe. For example,

---

[20] Steve Hill. *Spiritual Avalanche*. Lake Mary, Florida: Charisma House Publishers. 2013. Author's website www.stevehill.org.

Germany has more Muslims than indigenous people. Same with Secularism and Humanism in America or America would not be headed in the direction of socialism.

Many following Islam, regardless how biased it is, say unless the teachings line up with Islam principles, as emphasized by the Quran, it is to be considered false. If you think about what was just said from a Christians point of view, then you can understand the attachment Muslims have to Islam, the Quran, and Allah. See if you don't agree. "Many following Christianity, regardless how biased it is, say unless the teachings line up with Christian principles as emphasized by the Bible, it is to be considered false." Am I right? Do not Christians have the same attachment to Christianity, the Bible, and the Creator God as do Muslims to Islam Muhammad and Allah?

Can you see how hard it is for a Muslim to convert, or even to stop following the Quran and praising Allah? I heard Doug Batchelor of Amazing Facts say the other day, it is found in the Quran that clear water (Islam) and saltwater (Christianity) do not mix. True. I believe he was discussing Chrislam realizing it would never work. Fair analogy considering it is Islam's destiny to remove the saltwater from the Middle East followed by the determination to purge it from the face of the earth. According to them that will be accomplished by all Muslims supporting those who are referred to as "Merciless Avengers." The following epitomizes just who might fit the description of a cold-blooded killer and receive rewards for serving Allah after they die. The "misunderstood" Muslims.

X

Merciless Avengers

SINCE AMERICA IS THE LAST bastille of a Judeo-Christian society, the information covered so far is hard to accept as it might mean a clash of cultures, as well as societies, religions, and even the God we worship. Again, one cannot praise and worship the Creator God and the Muslim god at the same time, as they are extremely opposed to each other. One can only resort to appeasement in trying to accept the god of Islam in the hopes of living side by side as good neighbors.

For those who strive for appeasement, eventually the Islamic god would insist upon changing laws to sync more with Islam than conforming to the indigenous laws of the land. Or structures, or religion, or even societies embraced by the indigenous people of the country. We are witnessing this more and more as the refugee problem persist and more Muslims following Allah are spreading throughout the land. And the thought of another 9/11 can never be erased from our minds. Not since Islam has openly promised that another instance, perhaps even more deadly than 9/11 will occur. There is a trojan horse out there somewhere, and it is coming to America.

Being overly dramatic comes to mind, but am I? Is anyone being overly dramatic when they point out the facts of reality? And the current reality of facts does not represent imagined "realities." If I were talking about Islam only having a price on our heads that would be one thing, but when we include the politics that are tearing our country apart, one does not have to have a college degree, to have concern as to where our country as well as the world is going. All one must do is look around and see the condition of the world, and what one witnesses are very real "reality" facts.

Countries around the world seem to be awakening to the understanding of just exactly what Islam brings to the table, and the dangers imposed within that religion, but as we witness on the news almost daily, it may be too late for some to recover. America is teetering on that line. Without an understanding of just how dangerous extremists or radical some Muslims can be (and how loyal the silent ones are), or just how to defend against such an enemy, it may be an uphill struggle to pull our country back from the road that leads to disaster. Especially when one considers the decisions our government has been making. Decisions of appeasement that has set our country on, a road we seem to find ourselves pursuing at the expense of our country. What happened to leaving the next generation better off than the last? That is how much our world has changed in just a short period of time. Not just from the current Islamic threat, that appears to be silent for the moment, but from a government that embraces deception to achieve their goals.

Many believe we will have to live with the coming America as well as a degree of terror imposed by followers of Islam. And along the way we will have to contend with "lone wolfs" "want-a-be's and those who can be "brain-washed" as well as perhaps every other individual who can shout Allahu Akbar just before he or she pulls the pin to take life's and devastate families. It appears that we will have to continue enduring these individuals as we journey into the future while indulging in spontaneous attacks from time to time.

Unfortunately, acts that are designed to disrupt our peace of mind in what former President Obama referred to as a "whack-a-mole" terrorism situation. But these are not the hard-core avengers who kill children, rape women, and bomb churches, while killing hundreds along the way. In general, Merciless Avengers who destroy life by torture and death without the sign of a conscience.

Islam is coming to America and with it comes the constant threat of planting an Islamic flag over Washington, D.C. Those who wish to implement sharia law within our judicial system, those who are driven by the desire to blow us up and behead us as infidels. Yep, the future may not be very pleasant Sparky, but it appears to be our future. However, everything revealed leads Christians closer to being with Christ, as He says, "for the time is at hand." (Rev. 1:3: NIV). And as Patrick Herron says: We've been warned.[21] By the signs of the times, we have been warned.

The Middle East has been a powder keg ready to explode for some time, not only militarily, but exploding their ideology upon the world stage with more determination than ever before in the history of the world. Iran is disrupting the world with the intent of pushing Israel into the sea motivated from the desire to establish a caliphate state for their messiah as world ruler to rule from the seat of David in the city of Jerusalem.

To accomplish that task, we see "saber rattling" from time to time by various groups within, and around, the Middle East by the threats of Islam. Israel takes these threats seriously, even providing its citizens with gas masks from time to time. America should take those who follow Allah that seriously. Al-Qaeda is always threatening to blow up something, anything, anywhere. Another 9/11 could be on the horizon perpetrated by jihadist—fundamentalist Islamic extremist, or as some may refer to them as, Merciless Avengers, the "other guys," who are just waiting in the wings to unleash terror upon Americans.

The Islamic Jihadist—avengers

Jihadist, a cold-blooded killer. There just isn't any nicer way of describing a Jihadist. What does it mean to be a jihadist? Someone

---

[21] Patrick Heron. *Apocalypse Soon*. Published in Gresham, Oregon: Anomalos Publishing. 2007.

willing to die for the cause of Islam and take someone with them. It appears to many that those who might be described as extreme jihadist just simply adhere to the teachings of Muhammad more faithfully, more verbatim than perhaps other Muslims. But the goal of all seems to be the destruction of Israel and the riddance of infidels. And as Professor Samuel P. Huntington points out, Muslims have pursued this agenda for fourteen hundred years.

In 1998 Harvard University Professor Samuel P. Huntington warned Americans about deceiving ourselves concerning the true nature of the Islamic threat as he says, "Some Westerners, including Bill Clinton, [and President Obama] have argued that the West does not have problems with Islam, but only with violent Islamic extremist. Fourteen hundred years of history demonstrates otherwise."[22]

Have we been blind to the true purpose and intent of Islam as brought to our attention by Muslim theology for all these years? Perhaps we have just avoided the consequence of considering it. Or maybe still, we just never wanted to accept the fact that the unbelievable, perhaps even the inconceivable, would have the potential of coming to fruition in our lifetime. At least not to the level it has with the spread of Islam throughout the entire world.

There was the 9/11 attack on the United States that cost America so much and changed our-way of life forever. But prior to that, we cannot forget there was the terrorist attack against the USS Cole that killed 17 American sailors and injured 39 more; and the bombing of the American embassy in Beirut killing 24; or the world trade center bombing prior to 9/11 that killed 6; or the 98' embassy bombing in Kenya that killed 24. The list goes on and on leading many non-Muslims to indict Islam as a violent religion followed by many violent people.

When it comes to merciless avengers (Jihadist) spreading Islam throughout the world with little regard to humanity, that

---

[22] Hanegraaff, Hank. *Christianity in Crisis.*

is exactly what Iran is all about. Iran has been allowed to do just that since Iraq was removed as a threat, and Afghanistan is once again in the hands of some very bad people who are determined to destroy America and our way of life. For those deniers we have a stark reminder of current reality, brought to us by Ayatollah Ruhollah Khomeini of Iran (one doesn't get much higher than this guy):

> "The governments of the world should know that Islam cannot be defeated. [After twenty years America should be convinced of that reality.] Islam will be victorious in all countries of the world, and Islam and the teaching of the Quran will prevail all over the world." Benjamin Netanyahu must have felt the chill from that statement as he remarked, "What is at stake today is nothing less than the survival of our civilization."

When Saddam Hussain was removed from power in Iraq that action disrupted the balance of power in the Middle East. Without Iraq keeping Iran's nuclear program in check, Iran has been allowed to become, as described in the Bible, and brought to our attention by many futurists, "the king of the south." And now with the evacuation of America from the Middle East, Iran, with the support of China and Russia, and the billions of dollars they received from the Obama administration, and the billions of dollars of military equipment and technology given to Islam by the Biden administration, the time of concern for Israel is real, just as it is real for America. Although Israel seems to take it slightly more seriously than America.

A king the Bible talks about that will rise in the latter days to take peace from the world and many believe the Bible refers to Iran as that king. It's hard to imagine, but many futurists believe former President Bush was fulfilling prophesy when he invaded Iraq. Thus turning Iran loose to spread their ideology and deception throughout the world, thus fulfilling their destiny. And that is bringing forth a great number of those who would bring Jihad to our shores. A fair question might be, "How many Muslims are there that conform to the merciless side of Islam?" The answer to that question is answered by Michael Evans. That is the topic of the next discussion.

XI

Number of Merciless Avengers

IT MIGHT BE INTERESTING TO listen in to a conversation Michael Evans was having one day with Prince Mohammed Khalid regarding the number of radical Islamist who want to slit our throat. Would it be more politically correct to say eliminate us, or perhaps remove us from this earth? Regardless, those bringing jihad to our shores will slit our throat while praising Allah. That has been a proven fact of Islam.

Let's try to pinpoint the number of "foot soldiers" for Allah who would put their life on the line when called upon to do so. Michael Evans, author of *American Prophecies*,[23] was having lunch one day with the governor of Dhahran, Saudi Arabia, Prince Mohammed Khalid, when he asked about Islamic fundamentalists and the threat they and their fanatical religion could be to the West.

Evans said his words somewhat antagonized Khalid and he said, "Listen, your country is a lot more dangerous than ours. You can walk our streets at two in the morning and nobody will bother you. You can't do that in LA, New York, Chicago, or most of the big U.S. cities." Evans replied, "You're right, but that's because you cut off people's hands and heads in public squares." Khalid: "Well it works. What do you do? Put color television in your prisons and serve them Christmas dinner? And besides, don't insult our religion by exaggerating. Islam is a peaceful religion." Evans: "Are you telling me Islamic fundamentalist are peaceful?" Khalid: "No, they're not. But they represent no more than 10 percent of Islam."

---

[23] Michael Evans. *The American Prophecies--Ancient Scriptures Reveal Our Nation's Future.* Warner Faith-A Time Warner Book Group. 2004.

The other guys, the bad Muslims. Evans: "Excuse me! That really comforts me to know that only a hundred million or so people want to kill me in the name of their religion." Did you get that number? *A hundred million!* Wow!

It's really comforting to know that only 100-150 million or so people (currently the number is closer to 200 million with more coming on board every day) are walking around who want to do the same thing to you and me. And then have the Mujahedin al-Shura Council, which is a collective body of several insurgent groups, including Al-Qaeda, taking pride in claiming they were responsible for our "torture" and "beheading."

While dealing with intensifying tribulation from many factors, we are watching the beheading of people (mainly Christians) from, as Michael was discussing, a 100 million or so individuals who serve a different God than do Christians. Individuals who can burn people to death or slice them to death, and that even extends to children who are burned to ashes in front of their dads. Vileness never imagined is raising its ugly head upon the earth.

What many might be wondering, especially since 9/11, will we ever see better days again? Since 9/11 it is as if America has lost its compass. From the "shock and awe" President Bush gave us, America has had to take a long and hard look at who we are, and ask ourselves, what do we stand for? What do we want? We are divided currently and that appears to be a vulnerable position. That "shock and awe" moment seemed to be our great moment of fame as a military might. It has been downhill ever since. Former President Trump gave Americans a glimpse of hope that we were still great, but the adversaries of America won the day. Harm to America comes in different forms and from different directions.

Regarding the extremist who would do us harm as brought to our attention by Michael Evans, we could probably classify these hundred million, two hundred, maybe even three hundred million or so, as "radical Muslims, Avengers, Jihad's," who, like all Muslims following Muhammad, and the Islamic beliefs, as spelled out by the

Quran, have but one goal. Eliminate everyone not willing to bow before Allah. We might also believe that according to the latest survey as revealed on Fox News, approximately one percent or more, live in the United States and are awaiting a call from Allah. Anyway, it's conceivable to believe that the one percent mentioned could live and work in New York, Washington, Ohio, Virginia, Florida, throughout Oregon, California, Texas, and so on. It's perfectly clear they live among us just as Syed and his wife. Remember it wasn't long ago that Syed Farook and his wife, Tashfeen Malik lived among us and executed fourteen people and injured twenty, maybe even more, and Islam tells us they were only the tip of the iceberg.

To substantiate how things have changed, Charles Kimball in his previously mentioned book tells us Islam is now or soon will pass Judaism as the second largest religion in the United States. Wow! Think about that for a moment. There are more Muslims in America than there are Presbyterians and Episcopalians combined and growing every day. And that was prior to the influx of tens of thousands of Muslims after our exit from Afghanistan.

Charles also tells us that Christianity and Islam are the two largest religious organizations in the world, with some 1.8 billion and 1.3 billion adherents, respectively. Together, Christians and Muslims make up almost one-half of the world's population. Considering the approximately seven billion people (and growing expeditiously) living on this planet, it might behoove us to somehow figure out how to communicate with each other, otherwise what hope do we have as a society?

Kicking the can down the road or rearranging the deck chairs on the Titanic is only allowing Muslims who serve Allah more time to spread the religion of Islam across the world as well as infiltrate our country with their ideas, concepts, laws, and religion. Fourteen hundred years of an agenda is long enough to learn some history. But again…. What History? If we are now voting them into governmental positions, again, "what did we learn from

9/11? And all the other attacks perpetrated against America and America's interest throughout the world?"

America's new slogan should be "We Love Muslims." We love them enough to invite them into our country, even electing them to government. How soon we as Americans forget the pain, the sorrow, and sadness, and the grief they brought to our country with the actions of 9/11. But then, according to them, those were the "bad guys." The other Muslims. And if I am not mistaken, President Biden is only letting "good" Muslims into our Country from the Middle East, as was President Trump.

The spread of Islam is not a new phenomenon, however, Islam's spread into Western democracies is a recent trend and one that has been accelerating at an impressive pace. Especially with the recent Afghan refugee crisis which saw tens of thousands of Muslims loyal to Islam—while being opposed to Judeo-Christian principles—settle in our country. Again, I ask, how can two different ideologies that are loyal to two separate higher powers live together. Everyone who serves Allah say they can't.

And that brings forth the avengers of Islam to rip our heads from our body. Islam would declare war on the world if they thought they could convert the world to Islam. But that is not going to happen. If it could happen, most, if not all Muslims, those living among us, would side with their god (Allah) and with their brothers, (fellow Muslims). That is a fact. We know that as a fact because we, as followers of Christ, would do the same thing—side with the Living God and join with other believers.

It is the "angel of light." A spiritual entity who has only destruction on his mind as fourteen hundred years of Islamic aggression seems to be bearing out. OMG. Is that Islamophobic? But do I lie? I believe there are two sides to every story, so I listened to their side to see if I could understand how they justified Jihad—a struggle or fight against those opposed to Islam. I listened to see if, as they say, they can justify the killing of innocent people. That should be an interesting discussion.

XII

Can Jihad be Justified?

CHRISTIANS LOOK FORWARD TO LEAVING this world and going to a better place, but unlike Muslims they do not need to kill someone or be killed to accomplish that goal. Whereas Muslims want to change the world for Allah and anyone who is not on board with that objective will be eliminated. Sure, they will. Are people not being eliminated right now somewhere in the world at the hands of Muslims for not recognizing Islam as their religion and Allah as their god? And is the elimination not intensifying in certain parts of the world? We only have to look to the Middle East in general, and Afghanistan specifically, to find that answer.

But then, according to Muslims, Christians are accused of the same atrocities. They say we condemn Islam for doing the same things Christians have been doing throughout the ages, especially during the dark ages (between the 5th and 14th centuries). As a matter of fact, Islam throws the brutality of the Crusades (1095-1291) and the Inquisitions, probably beginning with the Spanish Inquisition (1478-1834) as an example of religious hypocrisy.

While some may be proclaiming Islam as a religion of peace, facts present a different story. But we already know that. They want to kill us and justify it by the brutality during the crusades perpetrated upon both the Jews and Muslims by the Catholic Church. Nothing against my Catholic friends but facts are facts. Anyway, the pope gave an indulgence (an exclusion from hell card) to all the crusaders forgiving their sins in advance for the atrocities that were going to be committed in the name of

"Christianity." Thus, sending forth the Crusaders on a journey of "justified genocide."

We are told in various books that the Crusaders were a motley mob of thieves, rapists, robbers, and murderers. Some of those who took up arms did it not for Christianity, but for their own personal gain, such as acquiring land, expanding trade, or recovering religious relics. But perhaps the biggest reward was a pardon from the Catholic Church forgiving any bad deeds committed during the Crusades in the quest for those rewards. And it didn't make any difference if a Jew or a Muslim was to pay.

Karen Armstrong puts it this way in her book, *A History of God:* "During the eleventh and twelfth centuries, the Crusaders justified their holy wars against Jews and Muslims by calling themselves the 'new chosen people.'" Catholics refer to this as Replacement Theology claiming the Jews forfeited being the Elect of God with their disobedience. Because of this disobedience the Catholic Church took up the vocation that the Jews had lost." Speaking of Replacement Theology as embraced by the Catholic Church, whether the Jews "lost" the promises given to them by God or not, promises that were sealed with a blood oath, that has been a topic of discussion for quite some time now.

I believe it was in one of John Hagee's books that I read where he alludes to replacement theology this way: "Those who teach that God has broken covenant with the Jewish people teach a false doctrine based on scripture ignorance and a narcissistic attitude." I believe most Protestants would go along with John. The Jews may have resisted heaven's grace, abused their privileges, and slighted their opportunities,[24] but the Bible tells us they are still God's chosen people.

The Crusades seemed to be the beginning of a war for dominance over the religions of the world, especially between

---

[24] Ellen G. White. The Great Controversy of the Great Protestant Reformation. Harvestime Books. Altamont, TN. 2017.

Christians, Catholic Christians, and Muslims. As a matter of fact, you might find this bit of information interesting. For some time now the Catholic Church has been reaching out to many, including Muslims, in the hope of finding a peaceful solution to the world problems. As mentioned earlier, there is something called Chrislam—the merging of Islam and Christianity—Catholic Christianity.

I say Catholic Christianity because the apostolic line of Christianity doesn't want anything to do with Chrislam. When Pope Benedict XVI spoke out against Islam it became his downfall as this was not the direction the Catholic Church was destined to follow. At the time of his removal, a potential battle was brewing that was creating a schism that the church did not want.

The schism was emphasized by the leader of the Salafia Jihadia Islamic outreach movement, Sheik Abu Saqer, when he said, "We did not need the words of the pope in order to understand that this is a crusader war against Islam, and it is our holy duty to fight all those who support the Pope...The green flag of Muhammad will someday be raised over the Vatican...and around the world and on the fortresses of those who want to destroy Islam... And it is our holy duty to fight all those who support the Pope." Wow! One could not be any clearer. Muslims have not forgotten the persecution inflected upon them during the Crusades by "Christianity" especially Catholicism.

Anyway, those must have been intimidating words to the Catholic leaders, as shortly thereafter Pope Benedict XVI was history. Pope Francis appeared to be a better fit with Islam. That is according to a report on News.Com on March 22, 2013: "The Pope has called for the Catholic Church to 'intensify' its dialogue with Islam and with nonbelievers, condemning the 'spiritual poverty' of the developed world..." He said he wanted to build a bridge connecting all people. But as we have seen, Islam is not on board as they contend the Catholic Church is responsible for burning any bridge that might have been during the Crusades, and therefore Jihad is justified. I just thought you might find that interesting. While many might agree that the Crusades were a setback to Islam, as we have seen, it did nothing to stop Muslims from spreading across the globe.

Crusader Brutality

It has been estimated the death toll at the hands of the Crusaders were approximately one million men, women, and children. The knights of Europe, under the orders of the pope, slaughtered tens of thousands of Muslims, along with similar numbers of Jews and infidels on their way to liberate Jerusalem from Muslim control. It was this ruthless quest for power that began the push to remove Muslims from the Holy land, reclaim Jerusalem for Christianity, and establish once and for all their dominance over religion.

The Crusades were formed for the task of rescuing the surviving Jews, but mostly Catholics, from the brutal conditions the Muslims were imposing upon them, those who were barely surviving under Muslim domination. When the Muslims invaded the Holy Land, as we saw, they killed thousands of men and enslaved thousands of women and children. They burned the Churches and shrines and deprived the inhabitants of decent dignity, treating them more like dogs than people.

Most would probably say the Catholic Church had good intentions, but considering the brutality of the Crusaders, Christianity has been under a dark cloud ever since, and do not think the Muslims have forgotten that brutality. They have not. And have promised retaliation by removing every Jew, thus taking the Holy Land back and returning it to the Muslims and under Allah, the rightful God. It was Allah who was ruling over Jerusalem during the time of Muslim control. And it was to remove him, and those who worshipped him, and to liberate the

Holy Land from the oppression by him, that Pope Urban II put in motion the Crusades in 1095.

John Hagee tells us in his book, *Jerusalem Countdown,* "The Crusaders are often presented as holy men on the road from Europe to Jerusalem and back pursuing a righteous cause with the blessing of the pope. All for the noble cause of liberating Jerusalem from Muslim control. That is what most think, but nothing could be further from the truth." Hagee continues, the brutal truth surrounding the Crusades implies they were military campaigns of the Roman Catholic Church to gain control of Jerusalem from the Muslims and to punish the Jews as the alleged killers of Christ.

That's right. On the road to and from Jerusalem, the slaughter of the Jews was justified because of the teachings of the Catholic Church that portrayed the Jews as the killers of Christ and who are lecherous, greedy, and rapacious people. So says John Chrysostom (345-407), who was Archbishop of Constantinople.

Perhaps it was this mindset that allowed for the most unfortunate example of brutality in the name of Christianity, even looking back through history until modern times. During the time of the Crusades, one notable instance of cruelty brought to us by John Hagee in the name of Christianity was perpetrated by the Catholic Church, or should we say, those ordained by the church. Upon entering the city of Jerusalem in 1099, the crusaders trapped more than nine hundred Jewish women and children in their synagogue and burned them alive, while singing "Christ, We Adore Thee." Hey, if we are going to discuss how horrible the Islamic religion is to Christians, then we must mention the Catholic Church as well.

I would not have believed that brutality as a fact unless I read it from a reliable source. Such an absence of the awakening of the Spirit of God that comes with a born-again spiritual awakening seems evident. Hagee says this kind of action to impose a belief upon anyone is no different from a member of the Taliban who straps himself with a bomb and murders Jews. Or anyone.

While the inquisition was persecution by the Catholic Church against the followers of Jesus for advancing the written word, the Crusades were the last push one might say by the Catholic Church to establish dominance and retain control over what they perceived as, "Wayward people who embraced the evils of the world."

The Catholic Church in the name of Christ slaughtered many, just as Muslims do today for not conforming to a certain way of thinking. It must have been hard for the Catholic Church to realize they were on the verge of losing the power they had enjoyed for so many years. And the control that came from that power must have been intoxicating, therefore, they were not going down without a fight for dominance and how better to accomplish that than to reclaim Jerusalem and take down the evils of Islam at the same time.

So, in the interest of Christianity and all that is holy, the Knights of Columbus, the crusaders, marched towards Jerusalem with one thought, kill as many Jews and Muslims as possible along the way. During the Crusades if one killed a Jew or a Muslim, the God that rules over the Catholic Church would see to it that they got to heaven, by way Purgatory, if necessary, from the power of an indulgence. Again, a "get out of hell free certificate." Harsh words but am I lying?

The Crusaders Against Jews

The Crusaders were on a quest to kill Jews and Muslims, but why kill a Jew? They weren't bothering anyone. The answer seems to be the Catholic Church claim that they are the "true" church, (replacement theology). And they hold the Jews personally responsible for killing Jesus. John Chrysostom (345-407), who was Archbishop of Constantinople was the first to label the Jews as Christ killers and began an era of anti-Semitism. You heard that right—he has been quoted in his homilies (lectures) as saying:

> The Jews are the most worthless of all men. They are lecherous, greedy, and rapacious. They are perfidious murderers of Christ. They worship the devil; their religion is a sickness. The Jews are the odious assassins of Christ, and for killing God there is no expiation possible, no indulgence or pardon. Christians may never cease vengeance, and the Jews must live in servitude forever. God always hated the Jews. It is incumbent upon all Christians to hate the Jews.[25]

Many consider this period of Christian history to be a very hypocritical time. Since killings were acceptable to the Church to justify the end results during the dark ages, then why is it not acceptable now for Islam to use the same tactics to achieve their goals? That is a question they ask. Islam has always justified the war against Christians because of the war the Catholic Church brought to them, but it would have made no difference, they would have found something else as an excuse to justify Jihad (a struggle against nonbelievers).

But the time of the Crusades is an easy target for finger pointing and all of Christianity has suffered since. As a matter of fact, I read the other day where Ali Hammuda, the Imam at Cardiff's Al-Manar Mosque in Wales is preaching what ISIS is doing is legitimized by Christian history because of the pain Christians caused Muslims during the Crusades. And on top of that, as mentioned, the knights of the Crusades were offered an indulgence which at that time reserved them a seat in heaven should they be killed in the process of looting, raping, and murdering.

---

[25] John Hagee, *Jerusalem Countdown: A Warning to the World* (New York: FrontLine Publisher, 2006).

Maybe we would like to ignore that period in Christian history, but Islam has been unable to forget the pain and suffering that was inflected upon them during the dark ages of Christian history by many who were carrying the banner of Christianity. Again, it would have made no difference as it is their destiny to accomplish dominance by doing exactly as they have been instructed to do. That is explained to us in the Quran.

Pain and suffering bringing about subjection and domination as only someone with the lack of empathy can do. Or perhaps even lacking feelings or compassion. But, someone without the spirit of the true God, the Holy Spirit, a spirit that is alien to a Muslim, they cannot relate. Without the Holy Spirit, what spirit do they have? Looking at that question from a Christians point of view, most agree that it is the spirit of the "angel of light." Does the Bible not tell us that Satan will aspire to overthrow God? Does the Bible not tell us the goal of Satan is to kill, steal, and destroy? And currently, it appears that the "angel of light" is doing a good job accomplishing all three. And when one combines what the Secularist and Humanist are bringing to the table, well, "katy bar the door."

Many believe the theology of Islam will continue to spread bedlam and destruction every chance they get. There are two worldly spirits deceiving people, the atheist spirit, a spirit that is embraced by those who rely on their own intellect for the betterment of the world, and the spirit of Islam. Since neither will be stopped, the future might appear bleak to many, if not bleak, then certainly interesting.

When it comes to Christianity, we cannot omit the Catholic Church, (representing Christianity). in their quest for dominance, just as with the Muslims, it appears to many that it was nothing more than two bull rams going head-to-head to see who was going to be the most dominate. The Catholic Church for power, prestige, and riches, while the Muslims were, and still are, driven by a desire to please Allah. And in so doing, they receive life and rewards. So says the Quran. Same with a Christian, and they await the arrival of their Messiah.

Until then, until the coming of Christ to put an end to the madness, the mayhem, the turmoil, maybe even the anarchy, that is currently engulfing the world, we endure the coming future with cautious anticipation. There is a coming battle that was set in motion in the Garden of Eden and intensified with the birth of Christ and will be finished in the book of Revelation. Or, from a Muslim's perspective, the fulfilling of the destiny of Allah as given to them by Muhammad and recorded in the Quran.

Or, from a Secularist standpoint, until they can make America the way they want, there will be no peace. This morning I heard on the news that the FBI raided President Trump's home. Never in the history of the world, and especially in America, has the hate and disgust risen to this level. And their does not seem to be an end in sight. If anything, most only see the mayhem and anarchy as mentioned. As has been discussed on a couple of occasions, "if Islam does not take America down, then count on the Secularist and Humanist and those who share their values, to do it for them." And it appears that neither will be stopped until they have complete victory. Wow! Where does that leave Christians? Those who cannot accept either, as both Islam and the wisdom of this world are an affront to God. And because of this situation, the next chapter describes some of the peace that is being removed.

XIII

The Removal of Peace

NUMBER OF JEWISH TERRORIST ATTACKS since 9/11, Zero. Number of Christian terrorist attacks since 9/11, Zero. Number of Islamic terrorist attacks since 9/11, 26,855. As we know, the goal of the "angel of light" as conveyed to Muhammad, and a goal the world is beginning to witness more and more as a fact, was passed down from instructions left in the form of the Quran. Those instructions were to spread fear unleashing intimidation. Intimidation that is designed to bring about stress designed to take peace from any society. Is that not what Satan wants? Is that not the job of the Four Horsemen of the Apocalypse? Was that not accomplished on 9/11—and subsequent acts since?

Those times should have been a warning as to the war we have now found ourselves engaged in with Islam, but because it is a different kind of war, a war we don't quite understand, a war we don't know how to deal with, we want to embrace those bringing us the war to find acceptance with perhaps the possibility of working something out. Even going so far as to invite them to be our friend in the interest of peace. That is probably not going to change, but, if we realize as American citizens by electing them to governmental positions and assigning them to committees such as the Foreign Affairs Committee, we are inviting the "angel of light" into the very soul of our country.

With a lack of understanding the consequences of Islam, as appears to be the situation with many of our leaders, we will continue being drawn into Islam by finding acceptance of their god, and eventually their laws, such as Sharia. A despicable set of rules we will discuss later. When the acceptance of Islam is conjoined with a lack of understanding as brought to us by the atheist god, a god embraced by the Secularist and the Humanist, we will continue being drawn into a godless world. If that be the case, and many believe it to be, then the world has arrived at the place described in the Christian Bible as the time of judgment, beginning with the Seals, then proceeding to the Trumpets, and ending with the Vial/Bowls as discussed in Revelation. It is the beginning of the time the Bible describes as "birth pains." A very unpleasant time for humanity in general but for Christians especially. Once again, I think of the frog sitting in the pot. The signs are approaching faster than many expected.

Other than it being the destiny of Islam to dominate, which is a goal that must be accomplished for Allah, Islam, in fulfilling that desire have spawn many Jihads. Cold blooded killers, who to them, Islam represents the only way of life. We know about the violence perpetrated by Islam, but can they defend the violence? They say they can because of the actions of the Crusaders, Islam can justify jihad against Christians Jews and Muslims because of the Catholic Church.

They hate the Jews because they, the Jews, consider themselves to be Israelites, the sons of Abraham, Isaac, and Jacob. It is that, but it also is the fact that the Jews claim the thread of redemption belongs to them. The thread that began with Seth, passed through Shem, and ended up with Abraham. From there, Islam and Christianity went in separate directions. And since both Muslims and Jews have a God, then one of them must go. And to Islam, the one to go is the God of Israel.

In Christianity, as well as in Islam, the thread of linage began with Seth, but when it got to Noah's kids, a parting of the ways began. The thread that led to Christianity was through Shem, while the thread that led to Islam was through Ham and Japhet, that is until Abraham. While both Christianity and Islam preceded from Abraham forward, they took different avenues. The thread that

80

led from Abraham to Muhammad advanced through the linage of Ishmael and then Esau, continuing until Muhammad. While the thread that leads to Jesus, the Christian Messiah, went from Abraham, to Isaac, and then to Jacob, who fathered the twelve tribes of Israel. And as they say, the rest has been history in the making. History now, and history that hasn't been written—yet.

Just a tad of history you might find interesting. Remember in the Bible where it tells us that God sent Joshua and Caleb to remove the occupants of Canaan and claim the land for the nation of Israel? A land that was occupied by the descendants of Ham and Japhet, and later, their descendants Ishmael and Esau. Land that had been handed down from generation to generation, beginning with Noah's kids, and suddenly, they are being attacked by their brother's descendants.

Now, it gets interesting. As we know, it was the Israelites led by Joshua and Caleb, who removed the descendants of Ishmael and Esau from the land of Canaan. Land Muslims would like to have back, but that is not going to happen, according to the Bible. Besides, they have Esau to blame for giving it away in the first place when he was hungry for a bowl of stew. That's how little his birthright mean to him. Muslims justify Jihad from the actions of Christians who they say follows the God who kicked them out of their homeland and disrupted their life's forever. That is according to them.

Muslims, like others, could say they have been persecuted throughout history, and most of the time it was a "holy war" of some sort. And surviving the persecution inflected upon Muslims by "Christians," and the "stealing of land" by the Jews, beginning with the land of Canaan, no amount of "peace offerings" will appease. Considering what we just read, the times that may be approaching will probably yield little in the way of stability.

The days that have been predicted to arrive, are going to arrive in such a manner that the moments will induce worry, stress, and anxiety. And we will have Islam, and maybe even our own government to thank for that. It appears we have no control over either Jihadist or the politicians who run this county. If Jihad was the only problem America faced, we could probably deal with it, but the drips of crime including homicides and the new trend of "grab and snatch.," are increasing daily.

The more that people can enter our country without repercussion, the more violence we will witness, that just makes sense. And, maybe I am wrong, along with a few million other Americans who feel it is all made possible because of losing control of our boarders, thus allowing anyone from anywhere to enter. Why is that? Why would America let into our country dangerous people? It is as if everything is happening by design. Leading us too someplace. We can almost feel it.

As a Christian, I can point to the book of Revelation and read about the unfurling of the first four seals of that book. Times in which peace will be remove and replaced with chaos. Many seem to think we are either in the times of the Seals, or we are approaching the time when peace will be challenged. The coming times are not going to be much fun for Christians, but they are going to be interesting, stimulating, and energizing as we continue following the path that both the Quran and the Bible has laid out for us. It appears that both indicate a new world is coming.

Muslims believe this and do everything possible to make it happen. And with the removal of peace from the world with the unfurling of the first four seals of Revelation, it is as if the occupants of the world are fulfilling their destiny. They, as well as the Secularist and the Humanist, are instrumental in advancing the world to the last few pages of the book of Revelation.

A book written around 1,800-1,900 years ago that foresaw a time in history Christians would be around to witness. What are the odds? And that is the releasing of the Four Horsemen of the Apocalypse upon the world to diminish peace and bring chaos, are we not witnessing that firsthand? Then we have wars and rumors of wars, conflicts, and rumors of conflicts. Are we not witnessing that firsthand? And let us not forget Mother Nature who has been assigned to bring its own stress and chaos. And then when one throws in the wrath of the judgments, as we are told about in the Bible, such as plaques, famine, starvation, scarcities, inflation, and death, they have the signs of the days prior to the return of Christ. A world that is becoming more and more under Satan's control.

America, as well as the world, seems to be approaching a society that calls good evil and evil good. A society where brother will turn against brother, both end time signs. Are we not witnessing that currently in America? It's as if the world is at war with itself, a war brought about, not only by the ideology of Islam, but by the ideology of liberals as well. The Atheists, the Secularists, and the Humanists of the world, those who disavow almost everything except their own wisdom. It's as if the current generation of millennialist have resorted to the religion of Zoroastrianism.

Knowing that it rains on the just as well as the unjust, we must accept the coming future trusting in the words of Pastor Charles Stanley as he tells us that we walk through adversity with the Holy Spirit as opposed to an unbeliever who walks through adversity with the spirits of fear. Or a Muslim who would constantly be calling, "Allah Akbar, Allah Akbar"—god (Allah) is great.

Christians are different and separated from the world by the Spirit of God, and He will always be with us. He will never leave us. But as everyone knows, trouble can happen at any time, rather it comes by way of Islam from the Islamic Avengers who bring Jihad to America, or by way of the atheist god who brings worldly wisdom to the table. When *religious* persecution comes, just remember, any coming persecution would probably pale in comparison with the Christians who were dipped in oil and used to light Nero's gardens at night. Only by the power, and the protection, and convection, of the Holy Spirit could anyone withstand that kind of death.

Unfortunately, when it comes to the violence perpetrated upon us and the world by the "angel of light" many believe it is only going to accelerate with the explosion of Muslim refugees throughout the world. And because of current times, extremist, those who wish us harm, are being allowed to relocate in America, as they are currently doing in Europe. I don't believe anyone blames most of the refugees as they are escaping homeland hunger and turbulence, and the fear of being killed. All brought about by the increased violence from a world that has become sick with anger. *Violence.* An increase of anger leading to hate in a world of emotions that are turning colder with each passing day.

Anyway, when called upon, Muslims have proven they are dedicated to their religion, along with Muhammad and Allah. Dedicated enough to sacrifice their life for the cause. Reminds me of the reformers who were willing to give their lives for what they considered "a cause" and every Protestant is grateful. Upon heeding this calling, which they are taught from childhood to prepare for, a Muslim will cross the line from "good Muslim" and become known as "the other guys."

The "other guys," remember them? They are Muslims describe as those who would kill and maim for the cause of Islam and when they do, they are considered jihadist, extremist, radicals, avengers, and so on, in other words not the "good" Muslims. I have a problem with the logic of "good Muslims" and "bad Muslims" as I believe a Muslim is a Muslim, is a Muslim, and they all accept Allah and commit to his instructions as delivered by the Quran. Probably that is why there is little condemnation from the Islamic community regarding any actions that advances the cause of Islam perpetrated by the "other guys." Actions that lead to conquest, but we are told by all Muslims, "not to worry when Islam comes knocking as we will be under their protection."

XIV
A Protected Chattel

WE ARE TOLD TO NOT worry when Islam is successful in their conquest. Muslims familiar with the Quran and the Hadiths have indicated that if Jews and Christians do not embrace Islam, not to worry as they will be treated as *Dhimmis* ("protected people") when the religion of Islam takes over. Charles Kimball tells us in his previously mentioned book, "The practical implications of *dhimmis* status have fluctuated from time to time and place to place in Islamic history, but the principle remains; regardless how much Jews and Christians may have distorted their revelation, [believing in the Trinity, and accepting Jesus as God's Son] they are to be considered legitimate communities deserving 'protection' under Islamic authority."

Traditionally Jews living in Muslim lands, (dhimmis) could practice their religion and administer their internal affairs but were subject to certain conditions. One, and perhaps the most important, is the required jizya (tax) to the Muslim government to avoid being beheaded. Dhimmis are prohibited from bearing arms or giving testimony in most Muslim court cases, as there are many Sharia laws which did not apply to Dhimmis. These were the conditions imposed upon the few Jews who began occupying Israel and came under the Islamic rule of the Ottoman Turks around 1517. The Muslims would control Israel for approximately 400 years. It was the British during World War two who broke the strangle hold Islam had on Israel.

With the destination of Islam to conquer, Dhimmis would be conquered people, the infidels of the world. That is who the

Muslims say would be "protected"—Really? How is that possible? The only way would be for infidels, those who are still alive, I say "who are alive" because as a Christian one would probably pay the ultimate price before bowing to Allah or paying money to subjugate themselves to Allah. For those who bow, they are to be treated as chattel upon conquest and now they are considered "protected people?"

Who's going to protect the conquered from Sharia? But even if we were protected, we would have to subjugate ourselves to the God of Islam or otherwise one might have to endure beatings a couple of times a day. According to those following Allah, subjection, oppression, and enslavement is the only way. Allah, along with his followers, will never consider an infidel as an equal, they are only chattel in the eyes of Allah, chattel owned by a mean heartless task master. It is not hard to imagine that the minds of Muslims are wired entirely different than others. But then they are taught from birth the life Allah expects them to live.

They believe what they have been taught from childhood, which includes beliefs that Islam is the purist religion and Allah is the only God, and Israel is full of pigs, and America is the Great Satan. They live and die with the mentality that it is Allah all the way. Only when Islam is in complete control, and everyone recognizes Allah as the one God, will peace exist in the world. Only when everyone is living in the world of Islam will peace reign supreme upon the earth. Every Muslim elected to our government in some capacity harbors this mentality as it is bred into them.

There is no middle ground, there is no negotiation or even discussion only appeasement until victory can be obtained. I believe I might have already mentioned this, but if not, Muslims live by the creed of "live in peace until you can achieve victory." Have you ever noticed the disruption that the newly elected Muslims are bringing to our government, to our country? Americans cannot see that the goal of Islam is to have America as a country divided, hating each other while verbally attacking each other, that is the goal of every Muslim elected to a governmental position.

Many Americans who have had enough of this hypocrisy, show their displeasure by addressing the issues. But soon realize it does no good as Muslims, such as Alexandria Ocasio-Cortez, Omar Rashida Tlaib, Ayanna Pressley, and Ilhan Omar, relish in knowing they are achieving the bidding of Allah. And that is happening right before our very eyes. It was Omar Rashida Tlaib who encouraged President Biden to give the thousands of Palestine's being settled in America—without proper venting, to be settled with very little fan fair to prevent any protest. Just something to think about. Considering those who are bring voted into government and are bringing their ideology, perhaps it is time to step back for a moment and rethink some things.

A few years back, just prior to former President Obama, Israel was strong enough to defend itself, as it has had to do on numerous occasions knowing America had its back. But today, today after former President Obama and President Biden, many have expressed fears for the future of Israel. Has not the Islamic community been strengthened in the last few years to become a real threat to Israel? Has our government not been treating Israel as an enemy? Obama did everything but turn his back on them.

A government under Obama and Biden has been a god sent for Islam. Have they not made terrorist stronger by giving them billions of dollars? That is the amount President Obama gave to Iran. Many say it was their money that was owed to them. Considering this, not one president prior to Obama touched that money as it would be released to an enemy of the State. Money that is now back in circulation to continue advancing the foundation of Islam ideology throughout the world.

Money that is currently helping to elect Muslims to positions of authority in America. Then visualize eighty-five, maybe even eight-six billion dollars' worth of the best military equipment money can buy given—just given, to the Taliban. A known terrorist organization that kills Americans and has threatened to destroy America and Israel. What is wrong with that picture? And, in addition to this, our current government is importing as many Muslims as possible to help in the changing of America. But not to worry as mentioned, we will be guaranteed protection.

Regarding that protection, remember that Islam is a spiritless entity controlled by a fabricated god controlled by the "angel of light." A god that will only accept those who will follow him, bow to him, and worship him. For those who refuse, well, they will fall under the "Spoils of Conquest." But again, we are told not to worry as we are going to be protected...owned as chattel but protected. Then on the flip side of that coin, the conquest by the atheist god—the antichrist, will demand everyone bow to him or face death. As all Christians know, he will demand our loyalty to the point of exterminating anyone who refuses, same as Islam.

At least they both will give us a chance to live, the only concession we would have to make would be to acknowledge either the Islamic god or the atheist god, depending upon which god is in control. They both demand total loyalty and worship. For those who disavow the Living God, then a Godless world awaits. But then not to worry if the god of Islam wins, we will probably be treated by them as we would treat them. They tell us they are good people and good people are there for others. If that is the situation, then why does Islam discuss the division of booty upon conquering a nation?

The Spoils of Conquest

And so it begins, the downfall of America without a shot being fired. In addition to four high ranking Muslims currently occupying important positions in our government, referred to as "the squad," there are many more in various positions of government with more on the way. I understand there are currently 169 Muslims holding political office somewhere in the country, and more than 200 who ran for some political office somewhere in 2020. Islam, and all that Islam brings to the table, is sneaking up on us. Remember the frog?

Anyway, if our country ever gets to the point as Afghanistan, a place of arrival that is totally under Islamic control, I believe most Americans will consider that unacceptable. Or perhaps as socialized as Venezuela, or Cuba, totally under the control of socialism (communism, Marxism, and/or Leninism, or a combination of all). A country consisting of people, controlled by an elitist group of individuals, who are living the good life, while others struggle. If we find ourselves in that position, we have been instructed on what to expect. From the elitist we will know subjugation as we are told of bowing before a governmental system—sure we are. That is what the coming antichrist is all about. And a government that is helping to advance us to that time is working overtime in preparation.

Many might not be aware, but the world is headed to a place where our faith will be tested as never before. But then, we already knew that. We are told not to do certain things and a Christian understands those things. And because we do, we cannot accept the wisdom, the worldly wisdom, embraced by liberals. And when I say liberals, I am talking about those who disavow God— Secularist, Humanist, and New Agers. Those who follow, as well as make laws and rules, by which people are expected to follow. Laws and rules from worldly wisdom—secular wisdom, and those who embrace it, even enforce it. Those who do not understand Christian wisdom. If they did, perhaps they would refrain from saying such things as we are about to read regarding, "what to expect."

Ironic as it may sound, I was watching a post on the internet from MEMRI TV a few days ago when I heard an Islamic Cleric say the following:

> In every war, there is a winner and there is a loser. If we win and invade the land of our infidel enemy, if we are the winners, it is only natural for us to impose the rules of Islam on the country we invade. According to the rules of Islam, all the people in that country become booty and prisoners of war: The women, the men, the children, the money, the homes, the fields…All of these become the property of the Islamic state.

And recently an Imam in the UK announced that when war arrives, Muslims will take women as Sex Slaves. Wow! Another difference in the beliefs of a Muslim and a Christian and the books they follow. As we have seen, the Quran is entirely different than the Bible. Yet, you may not believe it, but more than fifty percent of evangelical Christians believe the Quran and the bible contain basically the same information. They say the same about the Book of Mormon.

We know the books are quite different as the Bible does not tell infidels to rape and enslave people. Yet it might. Since I don't know every single verse, and it seems as if everything can be confirmed or opposed in the Bible if one looks hard enough, but on this issue, probably not. That is where Christians say the Holy Spirit is essential in leading, as well as educating, those who will listen, to the falsities of the world. Anyway, when the infidels are conquered, according to the instructions of Allah, it's okay to take women and children as slaves and rape them.

And that behavior is justified within the religion of Islam and discussed within the walls of many a mosque because of what the "Christians" did during the dark ages of Christianity. That's right, as was discussed earlier, because of the atrocities of the Crusades, many Muslims seem vindicated to pursue the course of violence when pursuing a quest in the name of religion and justify it with the brutalities they endured during the Crusades.

Skeptical? For a moment let's repeat what was said earlier and revisit that mosque in Wales and listen to Ali Hammuda, the Imam at Cardiff's Al-Manar where he has preached to many telling them what ISIS is doing is legitimized by Christian history during the dark ages. What was done during that period is hard history for Christians to live down and perhaps some of those chickens are coming home to roust. And by accepting Muslims into our country, as we are currently doing, it's as if we are trying to apology for the brutality of the past. But at what expense?

Perhaps it was that motive that initiated the following announcement from a city in California as they recently implemented a "Muslim Appreciation and Recognition Day." After which the Iman Ali Hammuda told his congregation that, "any appreciation and recognition day is irrelevant, war is coming against those who do not bow to Islam." That pretty much negates any good a Muslim Appreciation Day might do.

A Muslim Appreciation and Recognition Day? Again, inviting them to dinner embracing the thought that someday they will like us when they get to know us. Unfortunately, it doesn't have anything to do with how we think, it's how Muslims think, and they think in terms of enlightenment, or probably entitlement would be a better word, as brought to them by Allah and the Quran. And that thinking already has them salivating and splitting up the booty.

It took only fourteen hundred years but now Islam is closer to world domination than many might realize. The same applies to how close Secularist and Humanist have brought America to having our freedom limited. Atheists have goals, and like Muslims, they will never give up as they feel the future, and the control of that future is their destiny. All this finds' Christians caught in the middle, as if in a vise. But not to worry, the pursuit of world domination by the "angel of light" will eventually end with the coming of Christ. But until then, many, mostly Christians, would say, "katy bar the door."

But until then Islam and the atheist god will continue pursuing their goals of conquest at any cost. Of course, they each have their own agenda. The agenda of Islam being to conquer and only those who participate in jihad, along with those who make jihad possible, will share in the treasures of the conquered. And to share in that victory doesn't mean everyone has to blow themselves up to receive rewards, it could mean loading the bomb, or perhaps delivering the bomb, or supplying the money to make the bomb, and so on. And for that matter, even helping in the efforts by deflecting away from infidels the dangers of Islam and attacking those who expose those dangers. That is where the "bad guys" and "good guys" comes into play, and the word "Islamophobic" is used. Playing us like a violin.

According to the laws of Sharia and the Hadith the conquered people become the property of Islam and are to be shared among those who participated in the jihad, those who brought about the victory. Those who helped in overthrowing the governments of the world, thus eliminating all who bow to any deity other than Allah. There will be an overthrowing alright, but it won't be by either the atheist god or the Islamic god. We have discussed for a while a world of two God's, three if one throws in the atheist god, who seem to be vying for control. An interesting chapter that is coming up. But first, let us listen to Pastor John Hagee who conveys to us the determination of Islam to remove a polytheistic group of people.

Excellent Insight into the Future

And it begins with the removal of the Father, Son, and Holy Spirit, and the determination to bring that about. Wrap your head around this for a moment. If the followers of Allah are successful in bringing down America and convincing the rest of the world to accept Allah as their god, if that were to become a reality, and

Allah was the only God the world recognized, then the God of the Bible would no longer exist. The nation of Israel, along with the Jewish people, would no longer exist. There would be no more Bible, no more Christians or Christianity.

In other words, the God of Creation would be erased, eliminated, eradicated, and banished from the minds of people. If Islam was ever successful in their destiny, and if fourteen hundred years of history has proven anything, it has proven Islam will never stop short of total victory. The picture I get if that were to happen, as Satan wants, then I see God, standing outside of the boundaries of earth looking in, knowing He was defeated by the angel Lucifer, just as he had predicted.

Is that not what Satan has desired from almost day one? Has it not been his aim, his desire, to ascend above the throne of God? Thus, eliminate the creator God and rule the world from the moment he rebelled? That is why Israel must be removed. Israel will always be a reminder that Islam has failed in their destiny. It was about here that I found interesting what John Hagee had to say. He began by asking a question: "Why does Islam appear to have an insatiable desire to eliminate all who do not serve Allah?" And have unquenchable thirst to achieve such a victory.

Fair questions. If we could get to the bottom of those questions, then maybe, something could be achieved in bringing peace to the world. The very best answer I have found comes from pastor Hagee, founder of Cornerstone church in San Antonio, Texas. Pastor Hagee is another futurist who gives us excellent insight into what can be expected from the future in his book *Jerusalem Countdown*. Whooooo! Did you get that? Read that again, "Excellent insight into the future."

John Hagee, author, teacher, educator, lecturer, and an extremely educated individual regarding the Bible and the future as revealed by his afore mentioned book. An excellent book by the way that gives us insight as to why there can never be true lasting peace with the Muslim community, and why they MUST destroy

Israel, along with all infidels of the world. Some have placed him among the Prosperity preachers, but I have not found that to be true. And his son is also a very good pastor.

After reading what Pastor Hagee brings to our attention, I believe many may conclude that what he has said is perhaps the most profound information contained in this book, as it brings into focus the clash that is building between the Islamic community and the rest of the world and why that clash may be inevitable.

Hagee says in his book, "Islam believes the Prophet Muhammad taught absolute truth—that it is God's (Allah's) will for them [Muslims] to rule the earth. Therefore, if Islam does not defeat Israel, [along with all infidels] Muhammad and the Quran were wrong—and that's unthinkable. Therefore, they must defeat Israel." Wow! Therefore, they must defeat Israel, and we could add "all infidels" as well.

Many might interpret this as; if Israel survives, and if we as infidels survive, then Islamic theology that promised Islam the world for following Allah, might be viewed as a failure. And that is never going to happen. Otherwise, Muhammad might be considered a false prophet and Allah a false god. Again, that is never going to happen as Muslims are too dedicated to Allah for that to become a reality. So, by saying that, it would stand to reason the religion of Islam will continue to bring trials and tribulations to, not only America, but to the world as well. If for no other reason than to prove Muhammad was right about Allah being the "one true god" to be honored.

As John was saying, if Israel doesn't turn from their God and accept Allah, then they must be removed from the land they are occupying as it belongs to Allah. To accept anything different is to believe the Quran is wrong and that will never be accepted by a Muslim. Does Satan not want what Islam wants? Dominance over the world? Is that not the desires, goals, even destiny of Muslims who follow Allah and receive their instructions through the Quran. All given to them by a prophet, (Muhammad) who was himself following the "angel of light." The Bible tells us our battle is not with each other but with the spirits that entered the world in the Garden of Eden at the very time disobedience showed up. Recognizing this as a truth is what separates a believer from a nonbeliever. A Christian from a Muslim.

And to a believer, as mentioned earlier, the day will come when that final battle happens, the battle between good and evil. What does that mean? Well, if Satan wins, as he thinks he can, then the rejectors of God's Son will control the world, and, as all Christians know, that is exactly their goal. That is what the battle of Armageddon is all about. The battle, as some call it, the battle for all the marbles, World War III. A battle that began in heaven, came to earth by way of disobedience in the Garden of Eden. A moment that let evil into the world. But remember, without the disobedience in the garden, everything happening as it is, as well as in the garden, we, as Christians, would not have the opportunity to live forever. And personally, I have not met a Christian who did not want to live forever.

That is perhaps the main reason, well at least one of the reasons, Christians become followers of Jesus rather than Muhammad. Which of course, leads to a different God. Each are educated by the teachings representing the God they learn of and accept as truth. The atheists have no god except themselves, and the god of self-wisdom, as they are also guided by the "angel of light." Just who are these so called "gods?"

XV

Two (Three) Gods, One Space

THE THEORY OF TWO GODS is as old as the West Virginia hills, yet the concept is disputed by some including many Muslims. Discussing this subject is relatively new but is becoming more pronounced each day, as verified by the different actions perpetrated upon humanity by each God. And when one includes the atheist god/spirit, they have the "spirits" that are driving this world.

I believe most would concede that there are three spiritual entities who appear to be directing the world to the times discussed in the book of Revelation. The spirit of the Islamic god, and the spirit of the Secularist god, and each seems to be at war, a *spiritual war*, with the Living God. That will be the battle Christians will be facing, along with the *physical war* that many believe will involve Iran, Russia, China, and perhaps others, including America. The Bible tells us these wars are coming. While there is enough armament to destroy the world, that is not going to happen. It may appear to be coming at some point, but the Bible says that Christ will return before that occurs.

There are some futurist preachers telling us the god of the Muslims will be the one pushing the world to the brink of annihilation by their determination to promote Allah and bring everything under his lordship. While that may be true, and somewhat accepted as a reality within Islam, that thinking began to be challenged when Covid became a pandemic. The mentality of the world changed almost overnight. If anything, it placed the end in sight to those who perhaps were looking for signs. Signs that are becoming apparent to many as the signs representative of the times that appear to be lining up more and more with the signs as described in the Bible.

Gods of the End-times

If given the opportunity, the Secularist god followed by atheist will take control and continue leading the world to the times of tribulation—not the tribulation, as in the Great Tribulation, but tribulation that the world is perhaps beginning to experience. Tribulation that appears to some to be the time of the unfurling of the Seals of Revelation. The turbulent times that will continue to bring us closer to the return of Christ, but also, will be conducive for the coming of the antichrist.

The antichrist. A non-Jew, (otherwise the Muslims would not be on board) or a non-Muslim (otherwise the Jews would not be on board) coming to leadership from somewhere within the European Union. While the invading armies may be assembled in the EU, the antichrist could be anyone from anywhere, (opinion) who has tremendous leadership ability, and enough charisma, and talent, to lie and convince people he is telling the truth. To a degree, what our politicians have been doing to us for several years. Either way, some rough times lay ahead in the spiritual fight for dominance. The "angel of light" disguised as the atheist god, as well as the Muslim god, is at work even now, in elevating the times that are designed to bring about the days leading to the coming of Christ.

While there are many gods (Greek mythology proves that), there are only two (excluding the secularist god, the god of worldly wisdom) who have a distinct destiny to fulfill, only two who have been around since the foundations of the earth came into existence. (We see them manifested in the garden of Eden.) Many believe the future will culminate with the clashing of these two

Gods to see just which one will reign supreme. This supremacy altercation has been brewing since the betrayal of God, as well as humanity, by Lucifer (better known as Satan). Of the two Gods, just who will be the final victor? The Muslims say it will be Allah, atheists will lust after the antichrist, while followers of Jesus will maintain a study hold on Christ, and the God He introduced to them.

The Bible tells Christians we will know the signs of the end and how close we might be from the end by the current signs of the day. It tells Christians by way of the Holy Spirit that we will be able to discern the times, and where this generation fits into those times. Or as some might say, the various eras of dispensational periods of history that have led to the present. Which is the dispensational age of apathy. Times that unfortunately are being defined less and less to favor Christians. And if that be the case, as we know it to be, then the picture that comes into focus is the direction the world is headed.

To many it is clear, the closer we find ourselves to the return of Christ, the more tribulation we appear to be feeling. Are we not feeling some degree of tribulation that we have not experienced in the past? Just looking around at the world answers that question. Those kumbaya moments that many Christians, and the world in general once enjoyed, not long ago, I might add, and those days that produced those kumbaya moments are perhaps gone forever. That is sad to say, but as John Hagee and Hal Lindsey has said, this is perhaps the "terminal generation," the last generation before the return of Christ." And the Bible, as well as the unfolding of current events, seems to confirm what John and Hal said to be truth.

We are in a new phase of history where the current violence being perpetrated upon society is becoming more dangerous by the day. As Christians know, the God of creation did not send His Son into the world to create a world as stressful as the current one. Or did he? An omniscience God would have to know exactly where we are in history. While humanity may have taken a few twists and turns, the eventual destiny of humanity from Genesis to Revelation has always remained the same.

Much of the current world is beginning to recognize something or someone with higher intelligence (an intelligence many nonbelievers' question) is at the helm and leading us to a defined ending. Christians say it is the Creator God and Islam says it is Allah, while atheist say it is intellect—remember Zoroastrianism? A recognition of an exalted deity of wisdom, *Ahura Mazda* (Wise Lord), as its Supreme Spiritual entity. That appears to be the atheist god of the world.

There are many reasons that exist as to why the atheist god and the god of Islam, both brought to us by the "angel of light," cannot occupy the same space with the God of the Jews and Christians. Probably the number one reason is because their thinking is in direct opposition to each other. Probably everyone agrees with that. Even Muslims agree with that and proceed to explain just who the God of creation really is. At least, their version of who God really is, as put forth from the writings of Muhammad.

They put it this way; the only God, the one God to exist is Allah...period. End of discussion. But we already knew that. During Muhammad's search for what Muslims say is truth, a question about his God came up shortly after he left Yathrib. In answering the question, he perhaps gave the one and only answer deemed appropriate to him. An answer that eventually made its way into the holy book of Muslims, the Qur'an. An answer that explains why there is no god other than Allah.

No God but Allah

Muhammad described his God by saying to his followers; "Say, He is God the One God the eternal. He begot no one nor was He begotten. No one is comparable to Him (112:1-4). He is to be worshiped as the only God." Absolutely a true statement.

Christians would say the same about their God. The Bible tells us the Creator God has always been, even when there was no element of time, and he will be when there is no element of time once again. The alpha and the omega. Now if everyone believed that, we would be on the same page, and peace could prevail. But then, Muslims embrace the same convection and dedication towards Islam as Christians do towards Christianity.

Jay Sekulow[26] puts his spin on the situation of Islam's claim to a one God theory as he writes, "The Muslim belief that Islam's Allah and the Judeo-Christian God are one and the same stems first and foremost from the Quran itself, which commands Muslims to dispute...not with the People of the Book [Jews and Christians]... But say, 'We believe in the Revelation which has come down to us and in that which came down to you; *Our God and your God is One*; and it is to Him we bow.'"

As we have seen, that is not the case as common sense and logic dictates; *Our* God and *your* God as one God cannot be as that would indicate a misnomer exist. In conversing with a Muslim one day, he said both Gods are spiritual therefore they are one and the same. Spiritual or not, they are not of the same spirit. I told him a Muslim does not go to a Christian church to worship Christ any more than a Christian would go to a mosque to worship Allah. He never responded. Absolutely different Gods.

Remember, Allah would never share the limelight with the Christian God. That is being proven daily. Just recently approximately 40-50 Christians attending a church service in Afghanistan were murdered by Muslims. Each Christian was shot, twice, in the back of the head. That happened at the same time thirteen young American men and women were blown to pieces by Muslims. Now a question, "Would that be initiated by the Christian God?" One more, two Uganda pastors were murdered,

[26] Sekulow, Jay. *Unholy Alliance*. New York, New York. Howard Books Publisher. 2016.

one 25 and the other 22, when the two were beaten and drowned in retaliation for evangelizing Muslims. Again, would that be perpetrated by the Christian God? To say, *Our God and your God is one God,* again is a misnomer, a contradiction. The same God who wants to save us wants to rip our head from our body, that doesn't even make sense.

Jay in his book said something that is so very, very, true. He brought information to us explaining: How the Muslims' view Allah and his teachings. And how that teaching differs from the God of the Bible. He says, "understanding that may be the most important factor in understanding the Islamic world." True, so very true. Nabeel Qureshi, a Christian convert from Islam, and a scholar on the subject maintains that "acceptance of this idea [one God] dangerously subverts Christian orthodoxy in favor of Islamic assertions." Did you get that? A one God theory disguises the atrocities of a fabricated god.

How dangerous is the belief in a "one God theory?" Probably a couple of reasons can be mentioned. Qureshi affirms one by saying, it is quite clear, beyond the most basic contention, the contention that there is one Creator God to whom all believers owe their loyalty, and to Muslims, Allah is the only god that exist. Therefore, there is only one God to follow. And those following another god, such as a Christian, well you know.

That is the Islamic god embraced by all Muslims. And yet, *The God of the Muslims and the God of the Bible bear no resemblance even in the most fundamental sense,* which becomes abundantly clear after even a cursory examination of Muslim and Christian doctrines. Then Qureshi asked an interesting question. He asked, "why does it matter that they are not one and the same?" The answer seems to be the crux of what many are saying.

Then Qureshi answered his own question, "It is because the Islamic view of God, to a large degree, drives the Islamic world's thoughts and behavior. At the most fundamental level, [at the core of a society] a culture is influenced and shaped by the way it views

God. And so, the vast differences between the Christian God and the Muslim god cannot be ignored if we are to truly understand the Muslim world." That is so true.

That is why a concept of only one God is so dangerous. It detracts our thinking from the brutality of the religion of Islam by thinking a God, especially the God of a Christian, is the same as the god of Islam and therefore, if that be the case, how can I get mad at *my* God? Without a separation, how does one fight against the evil as brought to us by the Islamic god. Without a separation we would be fighting against our own God. That is why Islam embraces a "one God theory." That is why the two Gods must be separated. Finding a solution to live in peace and harmony would be a snap if we all served one God. The problem is, we don't serve, we don't worship, nor do we follow, one God.

One God persona

Let's look at what it would be like if one God served both Islam and Christianity. If there were only one God serving two religions, then he would embrace two spiritual entities and be guided by different ideologies. Depending upon which personality or spiritual entity was present at any given moment, it would be that personality that would surely determine his actions and thoughts, at least for that moment. As some may say, he would have a split personality.

Think for a minute, if there were only one God, and this one God had dual personalities, as well as dual characteristics, one would never know which personality would prevail. One day, the religion of Islam (which is instructed to kill all infidels and Jews) would prevail, and the next day it might be the message of Christ and salvation (his other personality) dominating. Or as Ted Turner of Turner Enterprises once said, "Maybe there is only one God who reveals himself in different ways to different people." No offense to Mr. Turner, but most Christians would find that unacceptable as that would imply God has multiple personalities...perhaps even divided deities. But then I believe I read somewhere that Mr. Turner has been overheard as saying, "Christianity is a religion for losers."

Anyway, it can't be one God, or he would have dual personalities, characteristics, and even interpretations that would come with accepting either the Quran as gospel or the Bible as gospel. See the problem? If it were one God with two personalities, it might be interesting to listen to his thoughts one day, thoughts that might go something like this: I hate infidels. Today I am going to instruct my son Jesus to kill infidels and prepare the world for my descendant—al Mahdi. I also hate the Jew who protect Israel. Today I am going to instruct my Islamic buddies to crush them. No, wait! I love Israel, I love the Jews, they are the apple of my eye, my elect, and I love those who love Israel, and I love the Christians who follow my Son, and find salvation through him. Oh, what should I do? What should I do?

That is not the mind of the God Christians serve. The Bible tells us there is but one God with one message...period. Only one God was there at the burning bush to talk with Moses, and it wasn't Allah. Only one God was there to lead Moses through the wilderness, and it wasn't Allah. Only one God was there to talk to Noah, and it wasn't Allah. To believe otherwise is to deny the very first Commandment God passed along to us when Moses was on Mt. Sinai taking notes.

For those who might say, it's a matter of interpretation, I say that could be considered if everyone was reading from the same book, then perhaps it could be a matter of interpretation (as we've seen in Christian circles). But since two "holy books" are used to instruct followers, the book they put their trust and faith in will be the one they follow, the one they will be inspired by, (especially if that teaching begins at a very early age). It is this teaching and those beliefs from different books that separates the ideology of

Islam from the ideology of Christianity and the god of Islam from the God of the Bible.

And it doesn't seem to matter which God one serves both promises rewards. But the ultimate reward of eternal life can only come through the Christian God, while Muslims say it comes from the Islamic god. Who ya gonna believe? One day, someone is going to be surprised. And yes, Allah promises eternal life and rewards to those who follow him, but can he deliver? Just as there are rewards waiting for Christians, there are rewards promised to Muslims for following Allah as we will see in the next Chapter. The Bible tells us that the atheist receives their rewards while on earth. I guess that is where the slogan, "whoever has the most toys wins." Is that it?

XVI

Islamic Rewards

AS WE HAVE SEEN THROUGH history Islam brings a lot of brutality to the table to hasten the arrival of al Mahdi, and for what? Especially since there are no guarantees in Islam as there are in Christianity when one becomes a believer. In Christianity faith is the main ingredient to heaven while in Islam it appears to be how much one sacrifices for Allah. That appears to be the deciding factor as to where one will end up. Whether we're in their land or they are in ours, killing Jews and infidels seems to be the only "guaranteed" ticket into the Islamic heaven.

Many may not know that, just because one is a follower of Allah, doesn't necessarily guaranteed passage into the Islamic heaven. Maybe into a lesser heaven but not into the main heaven, the Seventh Heaven. To be assured of receiving that ticket, the religion of Islam rewards Muslims for many things as we will see but killing infidels ranks the highest. Killing Christian infidels gets one a ticket into the seventh heaven where Muhammad resides. How about that? Christ says the guaranteed way to heaven is through Him, while Islam says the guaranteed way to heaven, is through being a Martyr.

Dying a martyr is encouraged by the Quran as the only "sure passage" from this life into the next. From this mentality comes an understanding that Muslims are not guaranteed heaven by faith, as is a Christian, rather they must show themselves worthy by their obedience to the Quran. And obedience to the Quran is what every Muslim lives and dies for. If they don't embrace Islam with their mind and heart, then they are not true Muslim, and as with infidels, they are only worthy of death. We saw that firsthand when America withdrew from Afghanistan. Muslims who aided America in any way were hunted down and killed by other Muslims. Christian, Arab, or Muslim, it didn't matter.

And what do they get for aiding America? Death. And those responsible for their death receive many rewards in the afterlife. However, to relish in that afterlife, it appears one must be true Muslim and believe in the destiny of Islam to the extent of dying for Allah. But one does not have to die for Allah to get into heaven. Dying is just the only "guaranteed" way. If one does not feel the calling to be a Shahid (a suicide bomber) they get involved in other ways. Muslims who continue doing the bidding of Allah by promoting Islam and promoting his ways. All done in the hopes this will make them worthy enough to be accepted into the Islamic kingdom.

Those following Allah and doing his bidding will be found worthy enough to make the Islamic heaven, and when they do, they will have rewards set aside for them. Allah promises rewards to those who volunteer to bring jihad to the infidels; as well as rewards for those who train those willing to fight jihad; as well as those who emotionally support those who fight jihad; as well as rewards for funding of jihad; as well as those who die for jihad, and so on. Those are just some of the actions that receive rewards under Islamic law. Again, unlike Christianity where Christians are saved by the grace of the Creator God, followers of Allah must show themselves worthy to someday meet Allah.

And, as mentioned, the highest honor comes to those who die in the process of killing non-Muslims in the promotion of Islam. They go to the seventh heaven where Allah and the leaders of Islam await them, along with seventy-two black eyed virgins. Then later they will be joined by the seventy relatives who were saved by the sacrificed blood of the Shahid while dying for the cause of Allah. Others who promote Islam in a "subtler" way probably go to one of the lesser heavens, one of the other six heavens, depending upon what they have done to promote Islam and the cause of Allah. Since Islam believes in a hell, we can probably assume those who miss one of these heavens goes there.

Jay Sekulow reiterates some of what we have been discussing as he says, "upon familiarizing ourselves with fanatical Islam, we find they are rewarded for blowing themselves up while killing infidels. Unfortunately for infidels, according to the Quran, jihad is among the good works that earn Allah's favor, and with that obedience comes rewards. In fact, [as mentioned a couple of times] dying in the way of Islam for Allah, is the *only* way to ensure acceptance into heaven." Perhaps even welcomed with the words, "enter thou good and faithful servant."

Anyway, the information conveyed to a Christian in the Bible, and to a Muslim in the Quran, assures rewards. Christians are told they can expect rewards from their God, and those rewards are not conditioned upon a Christian having to kill anyone to receive those rewards. The gift of eternal life is passed to a Christian by the grace of the God they serve rather than the brutality of the Islamic god as served by Muslims.

The Ultimate Reward

Most don't like discussing the negative side of Christianity or Islam and would rather focus on the many advantages of choosing one or the other. With this in mind, let's explore just what Muslims receive when they accomplish the task of following Allah, even to the extent of blowing up infidels. If they die a "suicide death," they are rewarded significantly. But probably the most treasured reward is the guarantee they have from Allah himself to instantly (others await in the grave) be resurrected into the seventh heaven, or as Muslims say—paradise, whereupon they will receive their rewards for dying a martyr's death. But we already knew that.

And the rewards are not bad for dying as a Shahid. For example, they atone for the sins of others as verified by Charles Kimball when he says, "they would go immediately to paradise and would guarantee a place in heavenly abode for their families as well." When was the last time you heard of a Christian blowing someone up to get a ticket to heaven? Not only for themselves, but for many of their relatives.

From early childhood Muslims are taught that it is a special calling to be chosen as a Shahid—martyrs willing to kill themselves for the cause of Islam. In fact, as mentioned, this is the greatest honor bestowed upon a Muslim, as this calling comes directly from Allah himself. Prospective Shahids from a very early age are told that when they accept the calling and become martyred in the name of Allah, they will:

1. Feel no pain or have any fear. The sting of death is removed.
2. They will not die, as all souls go into the ground awaiting the resurrection except the souls of the Shahids. They go directly to paradise, their own personal and immediate resurrection.
3. They will be honored upon arrival with a crown of glory that has a jewel of wealth of the world set in the center of it. Which of course sets them apart as the greatest of Muslims in the afterlife.
4. They will attend their own wedding with seventy-two black-eyed virgins for dying a martyr. They will be the guest of honor at the biggest event of their life.
5. They will pave the way for seventy relatives to go to paradise and be exempt from the horrors of hell. The blood of the Shahid atones for the sins of others. To encourage such suicidal deaths, especially among the Palestinian Muslims, the Palestinian government pays stipends to their families as the beneficiaries of a Shahid's death.

How about that? In the days that are to come, it appears we will have to continue coping with those who welcome martyrium to achieve their goals and accomplish their destiny as well as receiving rewards for themselves and their family. The Bible, as well as many experts convey to us that some of the coming times of turbulence and destructiveness will most likely be inflicted by those who feel it is their duty to bring about the wishes of Allah and become a Shahid.

Speaking of Shahid's, Charles Kimball[27] tells us in his book, a book recommended by a Muslim during a prolonged chat regarding the differences of Islam and Christianity. Despite the name of the book, it is a pretty good read. Charles keeps telling us he is a Christian, and he may very well be, but he is also a Muslim sympathizer. He seems to justify their actions and tries to defend Islam as a nonviolent and passive religion and describes everyone who serves Islam as "good people who are just misunderstood."

Charles tells us that: "There is a provision, however, [speaking of the destiny of a Shahid] for those who die 'striving in the way of God.'" Charles continues; "The Qur'an makes clear that those faithful enough to Allah go immediately to paradise: 'Say not of those who die in the path of God that they are dead. Nay rather they live' (2:154). Muslims have always interpreted these and related texts (such as Qur'an 3:169-71) as a promise for martyrs. Martyrs go directly to the seventh heaven, the highest realm, where the prophets, reside."

I don't know what to do with the information discussed so far as it so foreign to a Christian. Killing people to receive rewards to get into the heaven where the prophets reside? Wow! Where does anyone go with that information? Especially, when non-Muslims find out they are the ones being targeted for extermination just so someone can get into heaven and receive a reward. And as we saw earlier, there are those in our government who promote Muslim

---

[27] Charles Kimball, *When Religion Becomes Evil.*

doctrine and have sympathy for Muslims and their cause. AND again, what is their cause? Destroy the American way of life. Many say that America has been dumbing down for some time, and now the question might be, "have we dumbed down enough for Islam to become a reality and achieve their goals?"

That is some serious reality when one thinks about it. And as some might say, perhaps even too much reality. Especially when one throws in the desires of the Secularist and Humanist to remove God their way. If that be the situation, then the following section contains even more reality that many might find disturbing. When it comes to reality, I like how Bill Bennett and Seth Leibsohn put the consequence of ignoring it in their book *The Fight of our Lives,* when they said, "Reality can be a merciless avenger when betrayed." So true. So very, very true.

XVII

Are We Foolish People?

I COULD HAVE USED FEWER abrasive adjectives such as, unwise, irresponsible, ill-advised, maybe even reckless to describe the minds of many who defend Islam when we have such conclusive evidence that Islam is a danger to our society. Yet many declare Islam to be a decent, respectable, upright, moral, and conciliatory religion that has made several contributions to the world. I won't deny that Muslims have contributed to society in their own way, but that does not diminish from the goal, the destiny of Islam as given to them by Allah, and that is to one day live in a world dominated by Muslims who see themselves as overlords for Allah.

By referring to Islam as good or referring to any deed done by Secularist or Humanist as good, especially those that are contrary to the Bible, places us at a time in history exactly where God said the world would be as witnessed by the signs. I found it interesting as well as ironic how many non-believers, those who have denied the factual aspects of the Bible, are beginning to come to an awaking of prophecy that is unfolding before their very eyes. Prophesy that many thought impossible only a few years back. Just a couple of examples would be the "Mark of the Beast," and the ability of a government to enforce compliance to that mark as society demands.

In the interest of peace, there must be a way to eliminate dissention, and those who promulgate dissention, along with those rejectors of a better society. A society that has been developed for the masses. A society developed by wisdom, but secular wisdom, just as with the Zoroastrians. Remember them?

They exalted a deity of wisdom, *Ahura Mazda* (Wise Lord), as its Supreme Spiritual entity. A society without a Living God. A God who demands loyalty to Him and only Him. A God who imposes boundaries upon those who follow him. Boundaries that are an imposition for those who reject Him.

Again, it seems as if the world has come under the spiritual leadership of the "angel of light." According to Corrigan and Hudson, "some conservative Christian leaders have complained that Islam is incompatible with what they believed to be a Christian America." Right on! Examples of evangelical Christians who have expressed such sentiments include Franklin Graham, an American Christian evangelist and missionary, and Pat Robertson, an American media mogul executive chairman, and a former Southern Baptist minister. Many understand why humanity is incompatible with Islam and yet here we are, inviting them into our country.

I remember hearing Ron White the comedian saying, "you can't fix stupid." If we are lacking in some areas of understanding, and if stupid eclipses intelligence, what is going to happen to America? Personally, I don't think we're that foolish as a nation. A nation that is receiving tens of thousands of unvetted Muslims, as well as hundreds of thousands of immigrants. At last count, I believe it was more than a million, from several other countries, entering our country without knowing who they are and what lurks in their minds.

Perhaps we haven't come up with a solution to adequately address the Islamic problem while at the same time trying to appease everyone. When it comes to trying to appease everyone, in addition to lacking solutions for peace with Islam, it appears we haven't come up with a solution to resolve America's political divide that is turning brother against brother, mother against daughter, son against father, and unfortunately, lacking any sign of a solution to resolve this political divide.

That may be considered cynical, but I say cynical is to believe there is no solution to the problems facing the world. Many ask, how can there be a solution, or even appeasement, when there are so many views regarding what constitutes evil and what constitutes good? You know, that is a good question. Especially when one considers the words that are mentioned in the Bible describing the days when people will call "good evil and evil good." Considering that bit of information, how can there ever be a meeting of the minds? And without that, there will never be peace.

Just for fun, let's ask, the question; What constitutes right from wrong? Especially, when facts are ignored. The Christian Bible explains what is considered good as opposed to what is considered evil by pointing to those who follow the "angel of light," and do his bidding by embracing abortions, same sex marriage, gender transformation, pedophilia, and even spreading false doctrine. I'm sure there are many other abominations to God, but that is all I have.

According to a survey conducted by LifeWay Research, a research group affiliated with the Southern Baptist Convention, polled their pastors, and found that two out of three Protestant pastors believe that Islam is a "dangerous" religion.[28] Did you get that? Two out of three *Protestant* pastors believe Islam is a dangerous religion, meaning one out of three don't understand the ramifications of Islam. And I must assume Islam, as well as the rest of the world, considers the two of the three to be Islamophobic. In the words of those following Jesus: "Don't listen to them, listen to the facts."

Facts in the form of surveys that reveal the heart of Islam. Facts such as the 2013 survey conducted by the Brookings Institute where they found that 77% of terrorist attacks in the U.S. were initiated by Islam. Then in 2015 studies from the Institute for National Security

---

[28] https://en.m.wikipedia.org.

showed 99.5% of all suicide attacks were believed to be initiated by Islam. In 2016, of the approximately 11,072 terrorist attacks 452 were suicide attacks. Of the 452 suicide attacks, 450 of them were perpetrated by Muslim extremist, (Shahids). Once again, is revealing that information about Islam being Islamophobic? Maybe even racist? If so, I don't get the connection.

I was reading on social media the other day when a question was asked: How stupid are we? It was a post by Tom Carbone shared by Harold Clark on Feb 5th, 2018. The post went like this; We allow our government to flood our nation with Muslims, give them, along with multiple wives, welfare for life while neglecting our veterans, along with Americans who truly need help. When this is brought up as an issue, it never makes headline news as that talk just might offend Muslims.

Islamic immigration has been making their presence known in virtually every country in Europe, and it will destroy both Canada and the United States if we don't understand the people we are dealing with. Regarding the question, how stupid are we? Many would rather say "we are just uninformed." We are so "uninformed" that we'll stand by and watch the destruction of our country. And get this, for the most part, the comments posted in response to the question "are we that stupid" suggested we could really be that stupid. Go figure.

Defending Islam

Where did America go wrong? Am I being Islamophobic for passing several of these post on? After all, it paints Islam as a very destructive force that must not be allowed to come to America or Canada. Whoops, that ship has already sailed. Now we are going to live with the consequence. As I mentioned someplace in this book, people are going to die, the only questions that remain unanswered are, "who" and "how many?"

Perhaps the ACLU will get involved as they do from time-to-time defending Islam's right to challenge our way of life, as well as, what we say and how we say it. The *ACLU*. A group of lawyers who enjoy the freedom of America. An America that provides their children with good schools, nice neighborhoods to live in, and an opportunity to enjoy America as the land of opportunity, yet they continue defending many of those who would destroy the social structure of that land and the freedom that goes with that land.

That seems to be the ACLU's mode of Operation, although, they would probably view things differently. Anyway, this isn't about the ACLU or the CAIR even though the following by Chad Groening may be an example of what might lie ahead when the Council on American Islamic Relations gets involved. Just a sampling; Muslims win lawsuit when they are denied by companies to participate in 'fasting' and 'prayers' on the job. An Arab-Christian woman and critic of Islam says it is unfortunate that Islamic intimidation is forcing American companies to give Muslims special privileges not afforded to other groups.

Under a settlement of a federal religious discrimination lawsuit, up to 100 Somali Muslims who are current or former workers of a St. Cloud, Minnesota, meatpacking plant will receive a total of $365,000. That's around $36,000 each for being offended because the company did not make special arrangement just for them. The U.S. Equal Employment Commission filed suit against Gold'n Plump, Inc., and the Work Connection, Inc., an employment agency which handled some hiring for the plant.

Under the settlement, Goldn' Plump agreed to pay $215,000 to workers who were terminated for taking prayer breaks. And Work Connection, Inc., will pay $150,000 to workers who were asked to sign a form acknowledging that they might be required to handle pork, which many Muslims consider unclean. Brigitte Gabriel, founder, and president of ACT! for America, is outraged. "It is unfortunate that we are seeing organizations like CAIR, the Council on American Islamic Relations, working with these groups and representing these groups," "And a lot of corporations who do not want a dragged-out, basically a bad public relations campaign in the United States, are succumbing to this intimidation."

Mickey Mouse and Donald Duck, according to Gabriel, must pander to Islamic workplace demands as well. "We already see Walt Disney, for example, conducting training classes to their leaders at Disney World to teach them about being sensitive to Islamic demands, as well as prayers on the job, and fasting on the job, all because they have a lot of Muslim employees." Gabriel is urging the American public to stand up against special treatment for Muslims.[29]

Are we as a nation, standing up against this special treatment as Gabriel urges of every American to do? Some have, and because of the exposure of information as contained in this and other books, there is an attempt by Islam in the West to impose a "sharia-blasphemy" law to criminalize criticism of Islam. What we do with that information is up to us, but we have been made aware of it by people who are concerned. So yes, some are standing up to be counted.

It started when Saudi Arabia and other Muslim countries tried to pass a UN resolution to force Western states to criminalize criticism of Islam. Even the Parliament in Canada passed "Motion M-103" to condemn the so-called "Islamophobia concern" in preparation for a blasphemy law being imposed in Canada. According to the Sharia blasphemy law anyone who criticizes Islam, or the Prophet Muhammad, should be put to death. But we already knew that. It appears that we, more perhaps them, may have a "victim mentality" at this juncture. "Look at me and see how they pick on me and my religion." And folks, we fall for it.

Are we that fearful of what they might think? Or are we learning to live with intimidation out of fear. Have we reached the point of surrendering our county to Islam? Have we reached the

---

[29] Chad Groening - OneNewsNow - 11/26/2008 5:00:00 AM ⬛ ADD THIS ▪️💬🔖

place where liberals, those who seem to be embracing ideology that is more in line with what atheist want rather than what Christians want, and strive to achieve it for the many? Most Christians say yes, we've reached that point, while many others would probably say no. And let me throw one more concern into the fray of things. China.

For those who have not been paying attention China is buying up millions of acres of farmland. That is a good investment for them. That gives them access to raising food to feed their people. I believe with a little imagination; one can see how that might play out when China needs more land. And to most Christians, this seems to be what the "angel of light" wants, a divided Judeo-Christian nation with victory going to the godless of the world.

If so, then that might prompt the question, have we reached the mentality that would allow God to be removed from America? Most might have said 'no' at one time, but times have changed. A recent Gallop poll seems to indicate we are headed in that direction. Hopefully not, but it's going to be a struggle to keep it from happening. Radical Muslims use the blasphemy law to persecute anyone speaking out against the atrocities of Islam while condemning others for not listening to what Islam has to say. Are we listening?

Do we listen to Islam?

Are we an unwise country? Are we irresponsible? Or perhaps injudicious—imprudent, foolish, careless? Personally, I don't believe we are, although, I don't believe I am the only one who must rethink that position when I heard this administration was preparing to allow Muslims into our country. Muslims who have vowed to eliminate us and take over Washington.

Those are the ones who are being allowed into our country—with open arms as many might say, by our government. Regarding the question about being an astute country, let's take a minute to review the latest actions of Islam. Now these recent actions are only a few of the latest in a history that has extended over fourteen hundred years with little change as brutality is the ideology Islam embraces.

March 25th, Afghanistan, ISIS gunmen attacked a religious gathering killing at least 25 people and taking dozens hostage. Philippines, August 24, two suicide bombers killed at least 14 people and wounded over 75. France, October 16, a schoolteacher was beheaded by an 18-year-old boy who was offended when she showed a cartoon of Muhammad in class. France, October 29, stabbings, three were killed with one beheaded. Austria, November 2, five killed by Islamic extremist. Mozambique, a scenic country in southeastern Africa, November 10, Islam beheaded at least 50 people, turned a football field into a killing field. Executions and beheadings reportedly continued from Saturday to Sunday. That was all in 2020. Again, is revealing that information about Islam being Islamophobic, maybe even racist? Once again, I don't get the connection.

Looking at 2021 we find it to be no better. Pakistan, January 3rd, eleven workers (minors) were kidnapped by Islamic extremist. When they were located, they had their hands tied behind their back with their dismembered bodies scattered around the floor of the cottage where they had been slaughtered. January 21, a suicide bomber targeted a clothing market killing dozens. Inducing several protests to be launched. The US, the UN, the EU, and the Pope condemned the attack, calling it a senseless act of violence.

July 19th, a suicide bomber detonated his vest in a crowded market killing at least 30 people. August 26, ISIS claimed two suicide attacks killing 13 US service members and at least 170 Afghans. September 3, Muslims went on a rampage with knives killing six people before being shot in Auckland, New Zealand. I am going to conclude that there is an element of intimidation included in all these attacks and delivered with the message of hatred. There is no love associated with acts of brutality, or with those who perpetrate them.

The killings go on and on, even as recently as our departure from Afghanistan. A departure that saw 13 military members losing their lives days before they were to be home with family and friends. Young people who had their entire lives ahead of them who volunteered to protect our country and now we have abandoned the very cause they were fighting for. How does a country remove that from its memory? A memory that remembers the thousands of lost loved ones who sacrificed their lives, only to show the world that we can light up the sky with an awesome display of "Shock and Awe," followed by that large banner that read, "Mission Accomplished." And for what?

The fact that America thinks Muslims want to be our friends, and maybe on the surface they do, but under that façade is only an illusion perpetrated by Muslims themselves. A Muslim saying goes something like this, "make peace with your enemy until you are strong enough to defeat them." That was the situation at Yathrib, and Mecca. The most disturbing part of this entire situation is that America has bought into the fabrication of Islam as brought to America by the "angel of light." And all anyone can say to that is, *America*, we gotta love ya. You're going down, but we gotta love ya. That is something a Muslim might say, in jest probably, but the truth is, they mean it.

While every Muslim may not have hate written upon their heart, or want to die blowing up infidels, the question seems to be, how much support do they give to those who do? That is a question we as a nation, and perhaps the world, is trying to figure out while living with the intimidation of being killed or branded a racist or Islamophobic for expressing an interest in the religion of Islam along with those who follow Muhammad. In other words, what does Islam bring to the table in a world that is shrinking by the minute and cohabitation is becoming a necessity?

XVIII

Political Correctness

LET ME ASK A QUESTION, could the world reach the stage where Islamic conquest, brought about by those "whack-a-mole" moments, and perhaps another catastrophic event such as 9/11 or greater, be responsible for diminishing our freedom? Or the fact that Iran is closing in on having a nuclear bomb or two and have promised to use them—and many believe them. Or could that even be thinkable as a possibility? If our country every gets to that point, the point of Islamic conquest, it would indicate that an Islamic flag would be flying over Washington. If things get to that point, it will be the results of not realizing—*it is to that point Islam intends to take us.* While Islam is dominating in some countries, Muslims may find it a little harder to change the culture, as well as the basic structure of America, but they will never stop trying.

Although, with Muslims who follow Allah being elected to government offices, it might be only a matter of time until our country will change, not overnight, but again, like the frog sitting in the water not realizing it was continuing to get hotter. Just recently two Muslims were elected to Congress, Rashida Tlaib and Llhan Omar, who many consider their election to Congress, a rejection of 'religious bigotry.' That is a good thing. Right? So that proves there is found in everyone a degree of compassion, but there are those whose heart belongs to Muhammad, Islam, and Allah. Just as a Christian's heart belongs to Christianity. Everyone can decide what they will with that information, but the consensus on social media went like this: "We don't need

Muslims in congress who have the mentality of hate as they do." And to this the left went wild.

What is happening to our country? Are we a Christian nation or not? A recent Gallop pole indicated we are not. Many ask how Americans could elect someone who has such animosity towards Israel, and everyone who stands with Israel, as does Llhan Omar, when she supports the Palestinians. Every day she proves by the way she talks she harbors a dedicated heart to Islam. And let us not forget the voice of Louis Farrakhan who is an American black nationalist and minister who is the leader of the religious group "Nation of Islam" and considers Israelite's termites, and he seems to think of those who support Israel to be termites as well. We know who Farrakhan is, but do we know who Congress woman Omar is and what she embraces. The following should give a hint.

Recently a British Islamic terrorist seized a synagogue, took hostages, and demanded the release of Aafia Siddiqui. Fortunately, after a ten-hour stand-off, the hostages were freed, and the terrorist was killed. Siddiqui, also known as "Lady Al Qaeda," for her association with that terrorist organization, is currently serving an 86-year sentence in Texas for attempted murder of American soldiers in Afghanistan. And this is a friend of Ilhan Omar. Strange bed fellows for sure. But Ilhan Omar and her allies at the council on American Islamic Relations (CAIR) and American Muslims for Palestine have pressed for Siddiqui's release. Continuing to indicate how unjust the American Judicial system is towards Muslims.

Such flagrant bigotry that can run unabated in a Judeo-Christian country should be unacceptable, that is unless we are not a Judeo-Christian country. As we understand, Louis Farrakhan is a Muslim promoting Islam, and is someone who should be removed from our country, but since nobody is electing him to a government position, he seems to get a pass. Besides, the ACLU would make sure he had plenty of political cover on his side.

Richard Bennett

Someone who has the freedom to embrace Islam and denounce the very country giving him the freedom to do and say what he desires as he has political correctness on his side. What a country! But regarding Muslims being elected to office and being given access to confidential information, information that runs our very country, all most can say to that is, Wow! Especially someone who refuses to take the oath of office on a Christian Bible preferring the Qur'an instead. How could this happen?

Trying to find some answers I found, according to Google,[30] a total of 38,901 Muslim refugees entered the U.S. in fiscal year 2016, making up almost half, (46%) of the nearly 85-90,000 Muslims entering the country during that time. And according to social media, former president Obama relocated them in Minnesota's 5th congressional district where they played a big part in electing Ilhan Omar, the first Somali American Muslim and one of the first two Muslim-American women elected to Congress. She was not the first Muslim elected from that district however, that distinction would go to Keith Ellison who won a congressional seat in 2006 becoming the first Muslim elected to Congress.

Considering Muslims have different ideas, different goals, and even different ideology, ideology that is in direct conflict with Christian theology, seems to make peace hard to achieve. Considering that, how can harmony reign? And then there is the "offending" adjective, that is played by many who themselves are usually found to be offensive. How can someone not be offended? Secularist and Humanist offend Christians by their pro-choice stance on abortion. Just one among other stances that are offensive. And Christians offend atheist by reminding them there is a God, and there will be a judgment. Words of condemnation to them. All of this is occurring at the time the politics of America seem to have run off the track. Mainly, from everyone being offended.

---

[30] https://www.pewresearch.org,

122

The Nature of Offending

The Bible expounds morals, rules, and principles along with values that are embraced by both Secularist and Christians alike, and to a degree, by Muslims as well. But spiritual values and carnal values are entirely different. It appears many are saying it is easier to go along with nonbelievers (carnal values) rather than continuing to defend Christian values. The argument against biblical expression heard these days appears to be, "We don't want to offend non-Christians," or "we don't want to offend Muslims." Fair enough, but what about the rights of Christians?

Several years back, (somewhere around the late 90's) I remember a middle school choir during Christmas time having to eliminate the reverence from the song "Silent Night" so as not to offend people. Think for a minute, they, by this very act, offended people. That would have been a good time for Christians to stand up against such stupidity. It appears that currently, and for some time, America has been witnessing the repercussions from the apathy that was present that day, as well as many other days. How about another one. This one dates back to around 1960 when the renounced atheist, Madalyn Murray O'Hair filed a lawsuit for the removal of Christianity in our schools.

She fought years for the separation of church and State, especially within our schools. You might think that it would be impossible to remove Christ from the schools of a Judeo-Christian nation. You might think that, but is Christianity found in our schools today? If anything, most schools have removed themselves from Christianity altogether. I found it interestingly sad, how this whole thing started. One day while taking her son to school, she saw students in a classroom reciting the Lord's Prayer. She sued the Baltimore public schools for requiring students to read from the Bible and recite the Lord's prayer. She fought through the court system and being challenged by a modestly weak voice of protest she eventually won a victory in the U.S. Supreme court for the separation of church and state in 1963.

It appears these battles are brought about by a secularist world filled with many who disavow Christianity and lack an understanding of a creator God. Therefore, to them, it is in the interest of peace that they welcome Muslims into our country and embrace them and their ideology. All in the hope that one day everyone might work together to live in a world that promotes harmonious conditions. As we know, that will never happen if Christians continue to preach the word of their God. And it is that word that will, in many instances, get them killed, especially in the days that Christians say are not far off.

Not wanting to hear the word of God or relinquish any control over their life, they dream about the day they will be successful in stamping out Christianity, as that is the *goal* of the secularist world, while at the same time stomping out Christianity is the *destiny* of the Muslim world. Again, a vise many Christians could be feeling now, or at least feel an anticipation of those times coming.

As most Christians know these battles have been brewing for some time. Remember when the Ten Commandments were removed from a courthouse in Alabama by a secularist judge? Again, so as not to "offend" someone. Most fundamentalists understand the importance of not being misled by those who, through their worldly wisdom, follow policies of humanistic behavior. The kind of behavior that gives birth to deception, all the while being made to appear as justice and truth. Eventually, God's laws give way to human laws. Laws that are being substituted for God's laws.

When these issues were addressed during the days of Martin Luther at the Diet of Spires in 1529, which was basically a hearing against Martin Luther and the reformers in general, the reformers retaliated with, "Every secular government that attempts to regulate or enforce religious observances by civil authority is sacrificing the very principle for which the Evangelical Christians so nobly struggled."[31]

It wasn't long after this first incident that the country witnessed the removal of the Ten Commandments from another establishment. This was brought about by a Satanist wanting to display symbolism and idols designed to promote Satan. When he was refused, he sued to have the Ten Commandments removed as this was discrimination. Rather than pursue this battle through the courts or live with the alternative, which was to have satanic images displayed, the authorities gave in to the demands of "the angel of light" and removed the Commandments. Apathy. We are told as we approach the end of the book of Revelation, or at least the commencement of the judgments, the spirit of apathy would prevail.

In all fairness, I believe some of the Commandments have since been restored, but this was before Antifa. Anyway, that "sentiment" towards Christianity still exists. As far as secularism along with Islam go, they will continue to follow their own path. And in so doing, we will hear more and more "Happy Holidays" during the holiday season, and less and less Merry Christmas. Much less offence as Happy Holidays seems to offend no one. Happy Holidays wouldn't offend a Muslim, or someone from India, or an atheist, along with Secularist, Humanist, New Agers, and so on.

It appears the only ones who might be offended would by Christians. Christians are offended when they see an X through Christ at Christmas time. But, no matter, someone is going to be offended. We saw where Muslims said they were grieved, saddened which equites to offended, by having to live with Infidels. Infidels they would like to eliminate, is that not detrimental to America?

---

[31] Richard Maris. *Martin Luther—The Christian between God and death.* Belknap Press of Harvard Univ. 1999.

Just saying. And would I, as a Christian, or anyone who can see what is before them, be considered Islamophobic for saying that? Would talking about a Messiah that is different from the Islamic Messiah be out of line? Would it rise to the level that would warrant execution as is being witnessed almost daily among the Coptic Christians throughout many parts of the Middle East? And would it be Islamophobic, as mentioned earlier, to consider it ludicrous to even consider Jesus Christ working for the Islamic Messiah and executing those who will not convert to Islam and serve Allah?

If so, then put me down and call me Islamophobic because I call bull s*** on that thinking as does every Christian, and probably many secularists as well. America, as a Judeo-Christian country, desires to preserve the American way while living in a society that adheres to American values, and American principles. In other words, just being an American. If that offends Muslims— as they say it does, what then? Where do we go from here?

For the followers of Jesus who believe in a rapture, they know where they will be going, Amen? We discussed the word "offending" a few times in discussing Islam, and it seems like it was the concept of the word "offending" that led to what many refer to as Islamophobia. If that be the case, then, it might warrant a quick discussion regarding the word Islamophobia, as well as the connotation of the word, and ask if we, as Americans, are Islamophobic?

XIX

Are We Islamophobic?

AMERICA IS A COUNTRY OF big hearts, hearts with the mentality of "live and let live" and the freedom to choose the life one wants to live. Americans have welcomed Muslims into their country, accepted them as their own, even electing them to public office, and in so doing, Americans might find themselves the target of something they have trouble understanding. As far as understanding Islam, most Americans understand Islam but have trouble accepting it because of the brutality that is associated with the religion. It is when we question the religion or the Quran that we are faced with a word that was introduced to us some time back known as *Islamophobia*. Meaning a fear of Islam.

I saw an amusing cartoon the other day between a man and a woman that went something like this: The man said, "I don't believe that women have any rights, and I think gays should be hanged." The woman replied, "Wow, what a complete primitive a**h***! You must be a Republican." Hey! Ouch! That must have gone all over my Republican friends. Anyway, the man replied, "No, actually I'm a Muslim, and those are my religious beliefs." To which the woman responded, "Oh! I'm sorry! I apologize! I hope you don't think I'm Islamophobic."

Islamophobic. Many would like to pin that label on everyone who speaks out against or challenges Islam. Some people blame *all* Muslims who say they follow the religion of Islam for the many terrorist attacks carried out by extremist groups over the years, but are all Muslims to be held accountable for a few radicals who have gone completely off the rails? If we accept what was discussed earlier regarding the "good" Muslims" verses "bad Muslims" then "yeah." Call me Islamophobic for saying that, but facts are fact, and facts speak louder than words. Many would have us believe those perpetrating the acts of violence from time to time are the "other guys" the "bad Muslims." But then, as we saw, Muslim's serving Allah, praising Allah, worshiping Allah, do indeed get involved in one way or another to show him they are worthy.

We have the defenders of Islam, those who say, "terrorist groups have extreme traits of animosity, hatred, and violence, that have little to do with what most Muslims believe." Is that true? They say, "it is important not to blame a large group of people for what a small number of individuals have done." Is that true? We saw earlier where that was bunk, but many people think Islamophobia is created when a person doesn't properly understand what Muslims do, or the religion they embrace, and that the best way to combat Islamophobia, is to have a better understanding of Muslims and Islam.[32]

Personally, I can tell you, the more anyone studies Islam and the more they understood the goals of Islam, the destiny of Islam, and the reason Islam exists, as well as the one behind the goals of Islam, in other words, the one pulling the strings of Islam, the more they realize just how dangerous Islam is. The problem is many Americans do have an "understand" of Islam, the Islamic religion, and the problem attached with the ideology of the religion. They also understand Islam seeks to fulfill a destiny regardless of the cost.

Perhaps a certain amount of fear comes from a degree of uncertainty, but the main concern regarding Islam seems to come from those who follow Islam, who study Islam, who understand Islam, and refuse to be silenced by those who can't stand to hear the truth about Islam. The word Islamophobic also implies someone who might be considered a racist or has

---

[32] https://www-bbc-co-uk.cdn.ampproject.org.

racist tendencies—discriminatory, prejudiced, or chauvinistic. Nope! Nobody I know has racist tendencies, and I'm betting most Americans don't either.

Let me pose a couple of questions. If someone says they want to eliminate us, as those following Islam have said a couple hundred times, and when that bit of information is brought to the attention of the public, the informer is racist? Is that how that works? That prompts the question, "Is everyone Islamophobic or racist for identifying the facts regarding Islam? A question followed by another, "And then sharing those findings with others who just happen to have the same concerns as well?" Since those appear to be the questions, it might be a worthwhile moment to discuss them.

Again, not all Muslims have killing written upon their heart but there are those who do and would kill us, hurt our loved ones, our neighbors, our friends, and so on while yelling "Allah is great, death to infidels." And for those who are not yelling those words, they are aiding those who are. As mentioned, there may be millions of peaceful and tolerant Muslims, but that hardly means Islam is a peaceful and tolerant religion. A paradox that Hank Hanegraaff brought to our attention earlier.

Do you remember when Syed Farook and his wife, Tashfeen Malik executed fourteen people and injured twenty and maybe more in Sacramento California? When that occurred, the word Islamophobia came back to hurt us. A neighbor stated on the Fox News Network that she suspected something was not right with Syed but admitted she didn't report it for fear of being branded a racist. She could just as easily have said, "branded an Islamophobic" as others have. Friends this appears to be what our society is coming to, and this gives those who would do us harm a distinct advantage. Many may consider this to be a dammed if we do and dammed if we don't situation.

Again, are Americans racist as well as Islamophobic, for expressing how differently Muslims think as opposed to Christians? Or anyone for that matter? According to Muslims, the answer is yes, non-Muslims are racist. For example, Hank Hanegraaff says, "to impede Muslim citizens from practicing religion as they see fit is characterized as Islamophobia." We saw examples of that earlier.

If that be the situation, perhaps we shouldn't bring up the fact that Americans see hitting a wife, for any reason, despicable and certainly out of line to what is acceptable behavior. But Islam gives a Muslim man a thumbs up acknowledging the right to hit a rebellious wife who refuses to allow him "full lawful sexual enjoyment of her person." Why? "Because in accordance with sharia ordinances, *it is permissible for him to hit her if he believes that hitting her will bring her back to the right path.*"[33] I realize that is emotional information but another Islamic fact to live with.

If those of the Muslim linage, as well as those who are Muslim sympathizers, must pin the label of Islamophobia on someone, anyone, who expresses an opinion, then so be it. But then if that label is pinned on infidels it would appear, we are in perfectly good company. Remember Juan Williams was fired from NPR for just being honest when he said he got nervous boarding a plane and seeing two Muslim Iman's in full Islamic attire. Maybe that could be because, "THEY WANT TO KILL US!" And that is in addition to the desires of Secularist and Humanist who want to eliminate those who reject the wisdom of the world. And that would be Christians. As they, instead of relying upon their own wisdom as does the world, they opt for the wisdom of the Holy Spirit.

Regarding NPR, I picked up some interesting information while listening to commentator Andrei Codrescu when he was describing the return of Christ and Christian Theology. He described the return of Christ and Christian theology as "crap."

---

[33] Hanegraaff, Hank. *Muslim.* West Publishing Group. Nashville, Tenn. 2017.

According to a December 19,1995 transcript of National Public Radio's *All Things Considered*, Codrescu said "the evaporation of four million [people] who believe in this crap would leave the world in an instantly better place."

I believe most Christians would say Codrescu may be off a tad when he says only four million. Anyway, this same station fired Juan Williams for expressing his concern when boarding a plane with a couple of Muslim Imam's in full Islamic attire headed to an Islamophobia conference. Sometimes it just gets one wondering. I found out some time later that many people don't like Juan because his political views appear to be too far left for them.

But then, he did come from NPR which I believe is greatly supported by George Soros, or at least it was at one time. That speaks volumes, but when Fox news hired him, many thought he would be like Lou Dobbs who came from CNN, but he was more like the late Allen Colmes, Hannity's sparring partner on Fox News for many years. Rachel Maddow of CNN also came from NPR and has remained a very hard line liberal.

When anyone emphasizes what is happening to our country and how important it is for us to get a handle on the situation by trying to discuss the many problems, they put themselves in the position of being called a racist, a bigot, an Islamophobiac SOB, a Muslim hater, a conspiracist, and so on. What is being discussed isn't political, and it isn't about Trump or Hillary, or even Biden for that matter. I know those who support Hillary visualized a more kind and loving country. A live and let live environment that supports an individual's rights to do as they wish, think as they wish, and live as they wish, including abortions, same-sex relationships, gender changes and so on. I believe this is the mentality of President Biden.

Give Us Your Masses

One thing we know about President Biden, and liberals in general, is that when America said, "Give me your tired, your poor, your huddled masses yearning to breathe free" he took those words literally by initiating an "open border" policy. I don't believe anyone thought those words meant allowing into their country those who wish them harm, or those who unleash terror such as MS13 gangs, or those who desire to change our social structure, our way of life, and even the God we serve. As for the others, those who are willing to see America as a land of opportunity, then many would say, give them a shot. That's what America is all about. That is the America that appears to be on the verge of being dismantled.

I thought of the word dismantled, but I'm sure you can come up with a word of your own for America's current condition. Apparently after relocating tens of thousands of Muslims throughout our country without properly identifying them, and the thousands, if not millions of immigrants crossing our southern border, I guess we will find out who the bad guys are after they...well you know. Just as Nancy Pelosi said about the Affordable Health Care Bill, "we will need to pass it to see what's in it." They are saying the same thing now, "we will see who the 'bad guys' are after we let them into our country."

Regarding the Muslims who have entered our country over the years, they have an agenda as we have seen. An agenda that others don't. And when they form a majority, any country is at the mercy of the mentality of that majority. Even pockets of minorities, as we are currently witnessing, have power in America. And it is those minority pockets in the land of the majority, that eventually will change America. That is if the liberals don't beat them to it by turning America into a socialist country.

Maybe not today, or tomorrow, or even next year, but many believe that day is coming. The Muslims who want to see America become an Islamic state always seem to support a destructive socialist, (liberal) path for America.[34] A society consisting of a government that believes everything is made by cooperative efforts of the state with the help of its people and citizens. In other words, an authoritarian government that many have compared to China, but probably more like Venezuela. Some say without the coming of Christ, one or the other would eventually happen. Muslims who are elected to government, and or, the liberals. One or the other is on track to dominate. There are those who say that is not possible, and every American hopes they are right.

Would it have been possible for a Muslim to have been elected to a government position a couple of years after 9/11? Probably a very resounding "no" would have accompanied that question. But with time, here we are. And to carry this one step further, several Muslims have sworn allegiance to this country on the Quran. A book dedicated to a god who wants to destroy us. That's how far we have come in placating those who still desire to bring us another 9/11, and they will eventually make that happen. Is it Islamophobic to say that, even if it is just repeating their words back to them?

It's been a while since we have endured terrorism, but that doesn't mean it is not coming. Like 9/11, the planning is occurring even as we speak in a mosque or two somewhere. That, and the discussion of how to eliminate Israel the great Satan. That is the destiny of Islam, and it is the job of the Imam's to impart that information.

Those who elect Muslims to governmental positions must be aware of the dangers they are imposing on America. But then, as we are finding out, those who are voting them into governmental positions have the same desires and goals as those they are voting

---

[34] Socialism is a political, social, and economic philosophy characterized by social ownership and control of workers' and production, i.e., farms, factories, tools, and raw materials.

into office. In other words, the same agenda as the ones they are voting in. And considering the destiny of Islam, I don't know where to go with that information. Especially when disclosing it brands me as Islamophobic. Information that when one grasps the totality of what is being said that information should scare the hell out of them. And conveying that information makes me, as well as all others who think this way, Islamophobic.

Save those cards and letters and the post that show up on Facebook and twitter. I have seen them before. And, to them I say, sticks and stones, right back at ya, as many consider you Christophobic. We have differences of opinions; I don't see anyone denying that. And those differences cause riffs from time to time when Islam and Christianity come face to face, but that doesn't mean we don't like each other. Most Christians don't have a problem with Muslims as God's creation, just the religion they follow. And I believe most Muslims like Christians as well. But that doesn't change the fact that we have differences. As we know differences seem to make the world go around, but some of those differences are threatening to a civilized world.

The Art of Intimidation

One doesn't have to look very far to realize that there are many differences between Islam and most of the other religions in the world. Most other religions do not embrace intimidation with the art as does Islam. We know Islam is an intimidating religion, we live with that thought from past experiences. It was as if it took 9/11 to bring the threat of Islam to us in a very realistic and personal way. And Muslims have not stopped using intimidation as a way to win the war. When we, as a country, have been attacked as many times as we have been by Islam, then we are at war. A war we don't really understand, but a war we have been witnessing for fourteen hundred years. A war that will continue to intensify with the expansion of Islam.

Ever war has enemies. And for anyone to even think about a book alluding to the fact that Islam could be a fabricated religion bought forth by the "angel of light," or writes about "The Islamic Antichrist," as did Joel Richardson, places a death sentence upon that individual. Who would dare say those words knowing they are placing a death sentence upon their head? That indicates how well intimidation works. Rather the death sentence would be carried out or not is up to Islam, but as many know, the threat of death is not unrealistic. Remember earlier when it was mentioned about the happenings in France because of a drawing depicting a cartoon of Muhammad and some of the fallout from those incidents? Several died was the results.

When Denmark published the cartoon of Muhammad, in addition to burning children to death and killing Christians, according to the World-Net-Daily, nearly 1,000 Christian homes and churches were destroyed. They reported that more than 12,000 Christians have been martyred in the region since Islamic law was imposed in 1999. Considering this number was reported several years ago, a more accurate count would probably be somewhere around 25,000 to 35,000, if not more as the killings just seem to continue. But then, Muslims are under an obligation to Allah to protect Muhammad against those who would besmirch his reputation. Remember, Steve Hill said that more than sixteen thousand baskets are filled every year with heads of Christians, well we just some of those sixteen thousand. And don't forget the slaughter at Medina.

Anyway, Islam protects the reputation of all their esteemed. Conversely, they consider anyone who departs Islam a trader to Allah and must be eliminated. There is a word in the Muslim vocabulary *Riddah* that means apostate—a defector, deserter, traitor. A word that can get one killed without an understanding of its meaning, which is denying Allah's existence. Along with denying any part of the Quran, or claiming Islam to be a false religion, or leaving Islam, thus becoming a deserter, a defector, a traitor, all of which will get one killed. Based upon these conditions, Sharia law dictates those deserters, blasphemers, and all non-believers--infidels, should be killed immediately. Considering the contents of this book, it's probably a tad late to worry about that now.

The only thing I can say is that if I die mysteriously then everything in this book would be verified as truth. I have already been accused on twitter of writing a "hate filled book" having a "closed mind" and "lack understanding" from being "uneducated and misinformed." And any comments on Facebook elicit responses from the left, as well as from Muslims, as to how uneducated I am regarding Islam, while informing me how peaceful, and friendly, and law-abiding Muslims are. Especially, those who live in America. No argument there. However, the fact is, we don't really know how many of those living among us want to do us harm, remember the situation with Syed and his wife Tashfeen.

It may appear to the Muslim community I am being disrespectful, but I'm not. I'm only reflecting the image that is portrayed by those who follow the religion of Islam. A mirror (metaphorically speaking) has been placed against the religion of Islam and reflects what they claim to believe. According to the patristic tradition, humankind is a "free mirror." If we look at chaos, we will reflect chaos. If we look at light, we will reflect light.[35] We reflect who we are and what we think about most of the time. Christians think of Christ and Muslims think of Allah.

This book is not to besmirch the religion of Islam, but to educate Americans as to what Islam represents. And as an American citizen living in MY country, the land of the free, I

---

[35] Jean-Yves Leloup, *The Gospel of Thomas* (Rochester Vermont: Inner Traditions International, 2005).

should be able to do exactly that. But as with Rick Mathis and Joel Richardson, both of whom were vehemently attacked verbally, we subject ourselves to attack within our own country. How ironic is that? The more detailed, the more comprehensive, the more exposure one gives Islam, the more sever are the attacks.

It therefore is not surprising that many countries, as well as all Muslims who follow Sharia law, and that would be all of them, think that killing apostates—non-believers, defectors, deserters, and traitors as well as all who reject Islam, is not merely the right thing to do, but a religious obligation. Think about that, "a religious obligation." Based upon this information, one can only surmise the killings that take place by the acts of terrorism, will continue to escalate as there will always be a "religious duty" to remove those who don't accept Islam. Is revealing that information about Islam being Islamophobic, maybe even racist? Personally, I don't get the connection.

I just can't stop thinking about those dads who were forced to watch their sons being burned alive. Or a father who could kill his own daughter for disrespecting his religion by dating a non-Muslim. Horrific crimes perpetrated by ideology that has the potential of being unleashed upon humanity with more intensity and frequency than ever before. Over dramatic? I don't think so, although I am probably considered Islamophobic among the Muslim community for saying that. However, by now, I guess I'm thinking it goes with the territory. But then, I can't believe I am the only one who has a problem with anyone who wants to kill Americans.

There was the 9/11 attack on the United States that cost America so much. And we cannot forget there was the terrorist attack against the USS Cole that killed 17 American sailors and injured 39 more, while being docked in supposedly "friendly" waters. Then there was the bombing of the American embassy in Beirut killing 24. Or the world trade center bombing prior to 9/11 that killed 6. Or the 98' embassy bombing in Kenya that killed 24, the list goes on and on. Atrocities leading many non-Muslims to indict Islam as a violent religion followed by many violent people. And yet, we still want to invite them to dinner, even going so far as to extend an invitation to them that includes running our country. Only in America. Ya Gotta love it.

A Clash of Cultures

Whenever there is more than one ideology guiding people, you are going to have clashes as each side has agendas. Does the god of Muslims push an agenda to advance the cause of Islam as a religion converting people to follow their god, or as a political machine to bring forth conditions favorable to make Islam palatable? According to Former assistant U.S. attorney Andrew C. McCarthy as he attempts to answer that question says, "Islam is more of an agenda being pushed by the god of Islam rather than a religious organization." He wrote in the National Review; "When discussing Islam, it should be assumed that we are talking about both a religion and a political-social ideology." John Bennett a republican lawmaker in the Oklahoma state legislature in 2014 said. "Islam is not even a religion; it is a political system that uses a deity to advance its agenda of global conquest."

Even the iconic Pat Robertson told viewers in 2007 that "Islam is not a religion but instead a worldwide political movement." Some turbulent times seem to lie ahead from the brutal, and unstable conditions that will be perpetrated by those who believe in and follow the God of Islamic ideology. Ideology that is destined to bring about some powerful "clashes." Ideology brought to the table by the struggle for dominance by the two religions, three if one throws in Catholicism.

Think about this question for a second. A question Muslims ask; "How is a Muslim to live in a land governed by non-Muslims— infidels?" In other words, America. The answer: According to them—"eliminate the infidels." Remember, Islam must have dominance over the entire world, and in that world only "true and pure" followers of Islam are worthy of living. *"Only the true and pure followers of Islam are worthy of living."*[36] Wow! And when listening to what they preach, it is in their best interest to make peace with the citizens of America, their sworn enemies, until they are strong enough to defeat them.

Well, there it is. Now we have confirmation of the true destiny of Islam as given to them by a god opposed to the God of the universe. No equivocation thrown in, nothing convoluted. This is exactly what Muslims who follow Allah want to accomplish, and as John Hagee told us earlier, nothing but complete victory will suffice. Then the flip side of that comes from Christians who say that will never happen, but since approximately 1.8 billion Muslims alive today say it will, I guess a belief one way or the other depends upon which side of the fence one is standing. But Islam seems to insist we join them on their side of the fence, or we are not worthy of living, while infidels and Israel only want to live in peace on their side of the fence.

I wish I was wrong, but it appears that peace is not to be. Just look at the pattern of violence that has been exposed by this book alone. I realize everyone wants to believe Muslims when they say they are all about peace, but as we have seen, that is not to be. And even if it was, and they became a part of the fabric that our society has been built upon, they would be guided by Islamic law. And as we are about to find out, that just wouldn't work for Americans.

---

[36] Charles Kimball, *When Religion Becomes Evil. Five Warning Signs.* New York: HarperCollins Publishers. 2008.

XX

Governed by Sharia Law

SHARIA IS ISLAM AND ISLAM is Sharia, or Sharia is Islamic law and Islamic law is Sharia, however one defines it, Sharia is the religious law forming part of the Islamic tradition. It is derived from religious precepts of Islam, particularly the Quran and the different Hadiths. Legislative bodies that codified these laws sought to modernize them without abandoning their foundations in traditional jurisprudence. Unfortunately, with little success, as one might imagine since the consensus of sharia law mandates Islamic victory implemented upon any society where they have influence.

The Islamic revival of the 20th century, especially in the later years brought along calls by Islamic movements for full implementation of Sharia law, including reinstatement of corporal punishments, such as executions, crucifixions, beheadings, stoning's, or cutting off the hands and feet of an individual for stealing a loaf of bread. Although regarding stoning being politicly correct, I am told there is no Quranic verse supporting stoning in Islam, and yet, there is word of women being stoned to death from time to time. They say that stoning anyone strictly belongs to the Jews and Christians, while dipping people in vaults of acid belong to them along with mercy killings.

Many say Sharia law, which is fueled largely by fear, prejudice, and misunderstanding, cannot become a reality in the United States and elsewhere in the world as there are individuals and groups who are stridently anti-Sharia. As many have witnessed, the role of Sharia law has become a contested topic around the world when it raises its ugly head and attempting to impose it on non-Muslims have caused intercommunal violence in several places.

Countering Sharia law, as well as containing Islam, might be impossible. Especially with the progression of Islam through migrating to other countries. That is according to, of all people, the late Libyan leader Muammar Gaddafi, who boasted of the millions of Muslims already in Europe. Then he said, this is a certain sign that "Allah will grant Islam victory in Europe—without swords, without guns, without conquests. The fifty million Muslims of Europe will turn it into a Muslim continent within a few decades."[37] Islam also says this about America, without swords or guns conquest will prevail.

When we witnessed Muslims being sworn into government on the Quran rather than the Bible—pledging loyalty to Allah instead of the God of the land, one can only say, the conquest apparently has begun. And without realizing it, once again, we become like the frog in the pot, not realizing the temperature is getting rather hot. But if apathy and compliancy remain in tack, we will continue sitting in that pot. And while sitting in that pot, more reality of the direction America is headed, and what seems to be coming to America. More reality than many would like to accept or believe. Not only from Islam, but from the beliefs of the Secularist and Humanist as well. Many preach they are just as dangerous to our country. And why not, they are without the spirit that indwells Christians, just as many say Islam is a spiritless religion. Those are words one might hear from the Christian camp.

Any civilization that is becoming Islamic demographically will inevitably succumb to Islam politically. Had Gadhafi lived he would have witnessed more than one million immigrants, without an end in sight, being admitted into Europe. Especially being welcomed into Germany by Angela Merkel—dubbed by

---

[37] Hank Hanegraaff. *Muslim.*

Time magazine as "Chancellor of the Free World." No doubt Gadhafi, upon being aware of this, would have proudly donned the prophetic mantel.[38]

And let us not forget, Germany is the face of a nation in which the death rate exceeds the birth rate.[39] As a matter of fact, Muslims currently outnumber the indigenous population in Germany. I wonder if the German people realize how close they may be to losing control of their country. That will become a fact to them when Allah comes calling with instructions to enforce Islamic law, followed by citizens to abide by Islamic conditions.

Islam must embrace, as well as enforce, that mentality, or they are not following the Quran or being true to Allah or Muhammad. Of course, as we know, the people can refuse and pay a subjugation tax to admit defeat. But that would be no fun. As well as impossible for a Christian. But then, to be beheaded, or have my throat slit for not paying a tax, or accepting Allah as a god to be worshiped, doesn't sound very appealing either.

Gadhafi went on to say; "Europe is in a predicament, and so is America. They should agree to become Islamic in the course of time or else declare war on the Muslims." I don't believe anyone is holding their breath waiting for that story to make headlines anytime soon. Most of Europe, as with America, is swiftly moving in the direction of self-extinction—a death wish born out of birth control, abortion, euthanasia, and an ever-increasing elite population that, as with Muslims, have extermination on their mind.

Sounds like the future of America that is beginning to emerge as the young millennialist become adults. Many say we are becoming Europeanised. In other words, in nations such as Britain and Belgium, the native-born culture is dying out, and a rapidly multiplying Muslim culture is filling the vacuum. And

---

[38] Ibid
[39] Ibid

in so doing, they are bringing their culture with them, including Sharia law. It would be naive for Americans to think this is not possible within our own country. Maybe not tomorrow or next year, (remember the frog) but eventually, as we continue kicking the can down the road, with an "out of sight out of mind" mentality, Islam will be dreaming of planting an Islamic flag over Washington.

Maybe alongside of our own given their determination, and our willingness to accept Muslims into our country, by extending a hand to them. Electing them to governmental positions, making them feel respectable. Acts of acceptance that show how much we care as Americans to lend a helping hand to others in need. But then, that freedom comes with responsibility. Responsibility that has cost Americans plenty of money, along with much blood. Blood that has been sacrificed for our freedom and a way of life that until just a few short years ago, most thought would never end. How can America, unquestionable the most blessed country that has ever been, lose it all?

And Now We...Lose?

And now, without a shot being fired, it appears that we are losing our "way of life." Are we to say, those who died for our freedom, died in vain? How is inviting the perpetrators of 9/11, and the other atrocities perpetrated upon America and America's interest, not bring concern, maybe even a feeling of disappointment to the citizens of America. It seems to many that we are betraying those who lost loved ones fighting against those who want to bury us. How our heart, the heart of America, reached out to them. But now, just a few short years later, we are inviting their killers, or those who applauded those killings, to dinner. Is there not something wrong with this picture?

While discussing the planting of an Islamic flag within our country, if there is any doubt of this potential reality, then we need to listen to the words of the former president of the Society of Muslim Lawyers, Anjem Choudary, who, during an interview with Christiane Amanpour, said, "We do believe as Muslims, [not radical Muslims, not extremist Muslims, but 'Muslims'"] the East and the West will one day be governed by the Sharia. Indeed, we believe that one day the flag of Islam will fly over the White House."

Now there is a sobering dose of reality that many contend is getting closer with every Muslim elected to hold a position of authority within our country. And when it comes to reality, again, I like how Bill Bennett and Seth Leibsohn put the consequence of ignoring reality in their book when they said, ignoring the consequence of reality can be a real b**** with the potential of coming back to bite us. It went something like that. I might be embellishing it a tad, but you know what is being said.

You say, no way will we allow Islam to plant an Islamic flag anywhere in our country, but who is to stop them? And if they can be stopped, when does it start. Maybe not until the battle of Armageddon. Many see the fall of America as a reality that could be in the making even now, while pointing to the Christian Bible for conformation while a Muslim looks to the Quran for confirm that the end is approaching. Even many of the Secularist and Humanist accept that as a possibility. To perhaps understand how close we could be, one might point to the five empires in Nebuchadnezzar's dream, four have fallen with only the clay and iron empire remaining. And we are told of that empire's destruction.

Drifting from the subject for a moment, many believe that the fifth empire ends with us. An empire that began around 300 AD when "secularist-religion" was being introduced into the blood stream of the church. A church, the forming of which, is discussed in the book of Acts. The church that began with Jesus and was carried forth by the apostles and discussed as only the apostles could. Then around 300-313, the time of Emperor Constantine, Catholicism began to merge with the apostolic church and write theology that gave them a connection to the apostle church through tradition.

Beginning with assigning Peter as head of their church, even that was done by "tradition," where the Protestant church can trace their roots directly to Jesus through the apostles. And according to the book of Acts, the church that began to form on the day of Pentecost, was the church that preached the Christianity that can be found in most of the Protestant church of today. After years of Christian history, God used Martin Luther to break the yoke the Catholic Church had over the apostolic church. Eventually a split occurred when Martin Luther converted and received the Holy Spirit. God opened his eyes, or we would probably be Catholic or Muslim, or probably dead.

When, and if America falls, she will take the world with her, unless she is taken from within. While America can obliterate the world, we cannot seemingly protect our own country from within. When the terrorism of Islam that is to come, and come it will, with more frequency, and intensity, than any of the previous years we have witnessed. And when combined with the coming violence of Mother Nature that many say is to come, and come it will, with more frequency and intensity, leading many to say, "Katy bar the door."

Anyway, with the welcome mat hanging on the front door of America, a mat that many are taking advantage of, it appears that it is only a matter of time until America goes the way of Europe. And I believe many will find that the laws of the land will differ greatly from the indigenous laws of any country Muslims inhabit. Laws the world will not like, but with domination comes subjection and obedience. And as many may know, that would subject others as well as America to being governed by Sharia law.

Here is a test for those doubters. Ask the Muslims serving in our government if they would like to see Sheria implemented in America? I have no idea what answer one might find, but there is only one answer if they are serving Allah. And if they are Muslim, then they follow, serve, and obey Allah. So perhaps the better question might be, "Do you follow Allah?" Now we're beginning to understand what we as Americans are facing. But for now, an "out of sight out of mind" mentality works for me.

When it comes to Sharia law many found it disturbing enough in America to pass controversial laws placing bans on use of Sharia law by initiating the Nationality Act of 1952 known as the McCarran-Walter Act. An act framed as restrictions on religious or foreign laws (Sharia) that have become very controversial over the years. Lessons from the past unheeded today have the potential of taking us back to words that might go something like this; "to ignore history, one is doomed to repeat it."

There have been ongoing debates as to whether sharia law is compatible with secular forms of government, such as human rights, freedom of thought, and women's rights. All freedoms that constitute the soul of America. Because of this anti-Sharia stance by many, there are Americans who believe Sharia law cannot happen in America. They say Sharia law will never supplant the American legal system in any way. Well, if they plant an Islamic flag over Washington as they are determined to do, they certainly won't be asking our opinion as to which law we want to be governed by. And with more Muslims in our government who are dedicated to Allah, we could be closer than one might think to Sharia law raising its ugly head somewhere in America.

I don't know about you, but to me, all the infighting among the various factions of Islam leaves some confusion as to the understandings of Sharia law, and how Sharia has been adopted within Islam. As far as America goes, we understand that Sharia law brings a lot of restrictions, a lot of dos and don'ts, and it seems as if only Muslims who follow the Quran follow Sharia.

Meaning a different set of rules and regulations apply to Muslims than what might be customarily found within the structure of the country—any country—in which they may be residing. It's something when you think about it, when most immigrants migrate to America, they have always merged and became a part of America. But when Muslims come to America, it's as if America must change to conform to them and their wants. Exactly as we saw earlier. And when this situation is brought to their attention, they point fingers and go the Islamophobic route. Or maybe even the racist route. Any route to deflect from what is being said.

Muslims declare there are reasons for Sharia law in America. The Muslim American population currently residing in America is around twelve million and growing. These are patriotic American citizens who are law abiding, but who also desire Sharia law and vote for implementation of it. Because, as they say, not everything in Islamic law is covered under America's current system of jurisprudence.

A good example might be a Muslim who slits the throat of his daughter for violating Islamic law. Under Sharia he is not held responsible but under American law he is. Under Sharia it is permissible for a young girl to be raped, or perhaps endure "female circumcision," or female genital mutilation, but then they might still shoot her for just being a woman. As you can see, there is a lot of latitude that goes with Sharia that is not compatible with American law.

According to Islamic law even petty crimes are dealt with harshly. For example, theft is punishable by amputation of the hands. (Quran 5:38). Criticizing Muhammad or denying that he is a prophet or leaving the religion of Islam are all punishable offences by death. A non-Muslim leading a Muslim away from the faith is placing a death sentence upon his or her head. Think about that. Many missionaries from around the world are in the Middle

East to introduce Jesus. How dangerous is that? And yet, they still volunteer to go. In the Christian world, those are the true heroes.

Continuing with the shadow of death that hangs over Islam, a non-Muslim man marrying a Muslim woman is slated for death. A woman or girl found guilty of adultery is punishable by death, sometimes even by stoning. All anyone can say about that information is Muslims appear to embrace a very harsh religion of rules and regulations—pragmatic rules and regulations as opposed to a Spiritual society embraced by Christians. Pragmatism designed to subjugate and dominate rather than govern by the rules and laws of civilized societies.

Jan Michiel Otto, while sharing some thoughts on Wikipedia, identified four senses conveyed by the term Sharia in religious terms, legal, and political. Both delivered with discourse that is easy to understand for those who desire more information regarding Sharia:

> *Divine, abstract sharia*: Divine Sharia is God's plan for mankind and the norms of behavior which should guide the Islamic community. Muslims of different perspectives agree in their respect for the abstract notion of sharia, but they differ in how they understand the practical implications of the term. Probably the main difference between the various factions of Islam would be the differences that exist between Sunni's and Shiites.

Let me stop here for a second. We will return to what Jan Michiel Otto has to say in just a minute, but first, you might find this bit of information interesting as it provides some insight into the differences between the various factions of Sunni and Shiites. As mentioned, while they both follow Muhammad and Allah, and they both have a desire to push Israel into the sea, and kill us as infidels, they do differ from each other in other areas of their thinking. That difference has to do with who should have succeeded Muhammad upon his death. Differences that have existed between them following Muhammad's death in 632 A.D. at the age of 62 and have prevailed for almost fourteen hundred years.

Muhammad married a woman by the name of Khadija. A woman fifteen years his senior when he was twenty-five years of age. Khadija was from a very prominent family and was blessed with character, status, and beauty. She was influential in confirming Muhammad's prophethood and was one of Muhammad's first followers, one might even say his first cheerleader, followed by adherents of Islam like her cousin Ali (his second cheerleader) who did not descend directly from the linage of Muhammad, yet who later became Muhammad's son-in-law and the leader of the Shiites.

In early Islamic history, the Shiites were known as the "Party of Ali" claiming Ali as the only true successor to Muhammad, even though he was not a blood relative, and that issue bothered the Sunni's greatly. Since Sunni's believed only an heir of Muhammad could succeed him and Shiites believed otherwise. Considering this, the differences that exist between Sunnis and Shiites can easily be termed a family feud between Muhammad's blood relatives and his in-laws. I thought that was some interesting information from Jay Sekulow's book *Unholy Alliance,* along with a little help from Google.

They may fight among themselves because of the division that took place after the death of Muhammad in deciding who was to pick up the mantel from there, but they all rally around his religion. The question of the rightful heir to Muhammad has never been resolved, but then once again, that is a family squabble that spills over into the world. A world that embraces Muslims and many of their customs and traditions as they have been intertwining into the very fabric of the world, and much of it is appreciated. But when they try to intertwine Sharia law into a society, many draw a line by saying, "not in our country." Now let's return to the various understandings of Sharia law as presented to us by Jan Michiel Otto.

Classical sharia: The body of rules and principles elaborated by Islamic jurists during the first centuries of Islam. Probably the collection of Muhammad's dissertations regarding the new god Allah and what he brings to the table as well as how he brings it to the table. Some Muslims are likely to say sharia is the revealed word of God passed to them by Muhammad, perhaps this is more Shiite thinking while others might say sharia was developed by men from Allah's words.

Historical sharia(s): The body of rules and interpretations developed throughout Islamic history ranging from personal beliefs to state legislation and varying across an ideological spectrum of theology. As mentioned, Classical sharia has often served as a point of reference for these variants, but historical sharia has reflected the influences of their time and place.

It has been a proven fact that Islam will have influences upon any society where they take up residency. And with the introduction of Allah, a problem, a very serious problem to men's souls is introduced into the equation. It is impossible to live in harmony with someone who has been given a destiny and a set of rules and interpretations as developed and carried forth throughout Islamic history by the writings found in the Quran. Especially when those rules say we die, pay a tax, or become a Muslim. I believe many would say "That is the reality of Historical sharia."

Contemporary sharia(s): The full spectrum of rules and interpretations that are developed and practiced at present. Modern day Islam includes a developing culture that has been defined to include sharia law, again, to be implemented and developed and practiced. Many believe nothing will stop sharia law from being integrated into the judicial system of justice wherever Muslims have a voice. Even now I understand some judges have been asked to allow Islamic law to be used in determining the outcome of some. Perhaps "honor killings" would be an example. And let us not forget, judges have allowed government elected officials to be sworn in using the Quran rather than the Bible.

Islamic law covers all aspects of human behavior, and many believe it is much wider and deeper than perhaps western understanding has been able to visualize. Laws that govern the Muslim's way of life in literally every detail and, of course, it also regulates most of the business transactions required for daily living. There is no separation of church and state, or state and religion within Islam. Once again, we find out Islam is an all-inclusive religion that follows the primacy, the preeminence, of Sharia law.

While many judicial codes regulate public behavior, Sharia regulates most everything for Muslims. Public behavior, private behavior, and even private beliefs. Compared to other legal codes, Sharia law prioritizes punishment over rehabilitation and favors corporal and capital punishments over incarceration. Today of all the legal systems in the world, Sharia is the most intrusive and contains the most rigid restrictive set of rules ever conceived to govern humankind, especially women.[40]

In Islam, Sharia has enshrined inequality for women as a core value. Unlike men, Sharia does not allow women to have up to four spouses as it does men. Moreover, while sharia allows a husband to beat his spouse, there is no such provision for a wife. Nor can a woman initiate a divorce. Total inequality, and they commit additional crimes against humanity, crimes as we have been witnessing.

It follows that the Islamic conceptual framework is quite unlike that of a Christian nation in which law is based upon old English Law. According to Muslims, Sharia law has been abandoned and substituted by Western law, and because of this,

---

[40] www.billonbibles.org.).

their goal is to return, thus replacing American law with Sharia law, thus, placing the governing law of any state or country in the hands of its rightful owner...Allah as dictated by the prophet Muhammad. Did you get that? They believe Sharia law belongs in America, and that America has it wrong, and they are going to make it right. Islamic literature conveys that bit of information as a promise made by Muslims to Allah? Wow! They at least speak what is on their mind describing their destiny, the problem is, we don't seem to be listening.

There is a word in Islam known as *fatwas*. When analyzing that word, think of answers rather than questions. The answers are commonly referred to as fatwas and is considered wisdom only found in Islamic Clergy (Imam's) who are looked upon as carrying more weight than the opinion of a lay Muslim. Muslim scholars, known as faqih (experts in Sharia) are expected to give their fatwa (answers to questions) based on religious scripture as opposed to personal belief. Probably on the same order as the philosophers of early Christianity. This "additional knowledge" is what elevates a Muslim to the ranks of Imam. And the title for being the Grand Imam, referred to as the Ayatollah, currently goes to Ali Khamenei—Sayyid Ali Khamenei, the "Grand Ayatollah." We'll discuss shortly the influence this guy has within the Muslim community.

It is somewhat disheartening to know that there are so many adamant Muslims, (at last count more than one and a half billion and increasing daily) who adhere to the teachings of Muhammad and promulgate Islamic ideology that will only continue to spread. An ideology designed to bring discomfort upon nonbelievers (infidels) as prescribed by Islamic rules and laws. Incidentally, the concept of religious orders or *fatwas*, given by those known as *faqih* allows an individual, or a group of individuals, to justify killings. Something that is found only in Islam. Another reason for Islam to initiate Sharia law in America. To allow honor killings.

Honor killings

Every year many women are killed in the name of preserving the family honor. And according to Jay Sekulow[41] their "offenses" include dating without the family's approval, marrying a non-Muslim, or having an extramarital affair. There are honor killings right here in the United States. One clear case involved Faleh Almakeki of Phenix, Arizona, who was convicted of killing his daughter for refusing an arranged marriage with an Iraqi male. Then we have Rhaim Alfelaw who was prosecuted in Michigan for murdering his daughter for living an American lifestyle.[42]

I'm reminded of the story I read in Charles Kimball's book. He said: One morning while having coffee, he saw a young woman (19-20) being chased by a middle-aged man with a knife in hand. The man, who turned out to be her father, caught her by the hair, slashed her throat, and dropped her on the street to die. Despite feeling instant nausea from the grisly scene, I joined others trying to get assistance for the young woman, but it was too late. When asked what happened to the killer, nothing was the response—as it was an "honor killing."

Wow! Religious rules of pragmatism trumping the love for a child. Wow! As with you, I'm left speechless after reading that. Forget civil law, how about love, compassion, perhaps even caring? What kind of spirit would direct anyone to slice the throat of a son or daughter? When one understands the answer to that question, then they understand the heart of a Muslim.

Sharia Justice

It should be apparent that the law of Islam appears to be directly from the pits of hell and those who follow Islam and

---

[41] Jay Sekulow's book *Unholy Alliance.*
[42] Ibid.

promulgate Sharia law appear to be guided by that spirit, the "angel of light." This is obvious to every Christian residing on this planet. And when it comes to the law of Islam, now that Islam has breached our shores, we are probably going to be witnessing more and more implementation of this law. When it comes to the implementation of Islamic law within America, especially within our court system, more and more of our judges are being pressured into allowing Sharia law to be the deciding factor of many cases involving Muslim justice.

However, before deciding any case with Sharia law, or justice, perhaps the judges should be aware of the following: Islamic law (Sharia) that provides the backbone of the penal code and breaks many of its citizens, permitting and encouraging "flogging, amputation, and execution by stoning or hanging for a range of social and political offenses." Did you just hear that? How could anyone submit to that "overlordship"? And as we know, and as history tells us, people have and will again. All the while, speech is restricted, freedom of assembly is prohibited, protestors who demonstrate are tortured, and executions are commonplace. Are you beginning to get the picture? I told you Sharia law was insane.

Under Sharia law, there is no freedom of religion, no freedom of speech, no freedom of the press, no equal rights for women, and a non-Muslim cannot bear arms (that just got the attention of the NRA). Sharia law allows no freedom of artistic expression or freedom of thought. Islam wants to impose this upon America and its citizens, and to many it seems that the only defense we have is our personal awareness of the situation and the protection of our government, that was until our government began inviting them into our country.

Without an understanding of the depth of just how dangerous extremists or radical some Muslims can be, especially since they are entering our country under the facade of peace, many Americans are going to die. The question is…who? I guess we will have to just wait and see what destruction the head leader of Islam decides to bring to the table. To destroy and bring chaos to the inhabitants of the world is the goal of Islam. Remember, this is the guy former President Obama gave billions to for no reason. A guy that has vowed to destroy America and our way of life. Sometimes it seems impossible to know just who our enemies are.

XXI

The Head of The Dragon

OR AS SOME MIGHT SAY the "Religiopolitical" leader. The former Supreme Leader of Iran was Ruhollah Khomeini, also known as Sayyid Ruhollah Musavi, also known as Ayatollah Khomeini, who in 1979 came to power after being in exile. He returned to power in 1979 to become the religious leader over *all* Shiite Muslims. Prior to that time Israel and Iran had diplomatic relations with each other and shared intelligence. In other words, they were on good terms with each other. Iran was on good terms with America as well but that all changed in 1979.

In 1979 when Ayatollah Khomeini came to power, he let his presence be known when he instructed his followers to take captive the employees at the U. S. Embassy for, I believe one hundred and ninety days. I understand it was some fiasco when former president Jimmy Carter tried to rescue them. Anyway, it will be the Shiite Muslims who will be welcoming their Messiah, al Mahdi, and until then, it will be the Ayatollah Khomeini who will rule as the supreme religious leader of Iran and the Shiite people. The Supreme Iman is elected by the "Assemble of Experts"—Supreme Leaders who retain power over the people and direct their future, and probably will for some time to come.

Every Ayatollah since 1979 has preached the defeat of the west for being a cancer to Islam. It seems to me, that would require the elimination of Ideology, as well as the elimination of all who accept different Ideology than Islam. That realization has some Americans voting for appeasement, but appeasement never works.

In addition to the twenty years and three trillion dollars[43] wasted by America, Russia spent perhaps billions trying to remove the Islamic threat posed by al Qaeda. Both fighting the same enemy as well as each other. Russia was going at it very well and then we got involved. Why? I'm sure there are some politicians who could explain that. Perhaps, Dick Cheney, and Haliburton's involvement could be explained as well. Especially when it was alleged that American soldiers had been killed by their shoddy work.

I'm reminded of a power-crazy government consisting of many people who had too many toys and too much money, and one tremendous ego. That fiasco was followed by former President Bush's "shock and awe," followed by President Biden's embarrassing withdrawal from Afghanistan. These decisions have been costly to America. Many, especially Christians, know these bad decisions, as well as the ones being made by the Secularist and Humanist, those who are currently running our country, may one day make a decision that will cost Americans their independence.

Many said we were on the wrong side of history by supporting Osama bin Laden and they were proven right as al Qaeda brought us 9/11 just a few years later. If the goal/destiny of Islam, and especially of the former president of Iran Ahmadinejad, and the new president Hasan Rowhani, but more importantly, the Grand Ayatollah, is to destroy Israel. And in the process eliminate Jews and infidels in preparation of their returning Messiah, it appears nothing will be a deterrent. But do we as a nation, succumb to a heartless religion to accomplish appeasement? I believe Israel would rather destroy someone or something, or be destroyed, rather than say yes to that question. America, not so sure.

Since 1979 every Ayatollah has ruled the minds of Muslims who are taught from birth to accept the fact that they are superior to infidels and infidels are only to be used to advance Islam while

---

[43] Joseph E Stiglitz. And Linda Bilmes. *The Three Trillion Dollar War.* W.W. Norton & Company

being eliminated. I believe they say, "like cattle to be slaughtered." If they won't join us, I believe one can hear them saying, then they will at least pay a tax to show the superiority of Allah. And if they refuse that, then they must be slaughtered, but we already knew that.

I just happened to think of something I read in Timothy Ware's book *The Orthodox Church*.[44] *For the first time in our country's history*, the final push to eliminate Christianity, and those who follow Christ, is in full swing. A time of persecution as was witnessed during the power of the Emperors of Rome for not worshipping them and bowing to them. Sound familiar? Does Islam not demand our loyalty, even to be worthy to live? Many Christians believe we could be getting close to the days Timothy was talking about. First for refusing to bow to Allah, second for refusing to acknowledge the coming al Mahdi, and third for not bowing to the antichrist.

It has been said on a few occasions that Islam will not be stopped, as well as the mentality of the Secularist and Humanist, and the reason should be quite apparent. *Commitment.* Commitment is the root of Islam, as well as the root of atheism. Those who retain power, those who are committed to atheism as guided by the atheist god, or the concepts of Islam as guided by the Quran, find their roots in what the Bible defines as "sand" and sand makes for a lousy foundation.

In its history, the Islamic Republic of Iran only has had two Supreme Leaders: Ruhollah Khomeini, who held the position from 1979 until his death in 1989 and Ali Khamenei, who has held the position since Khomeini's death.[45] We find the etymology of the word Ayatollah is literally a sign from God. In Islam, Ayatollah is understood as "Sign of God," "Divine Sign of God" or "Reflections of God."

---

[44] Timothy Ware. The Orthodox Church. Penguin Publisher: New York, N.Y. 1993.

[45] en.m.wikipedia.org

A Committed Religion

Remember earlier during a search for the truth, a question about Muhammad's God came up shortly after he left Yathrib. And he responded with perhaps the one answer, the only answer, he deemed appropriate to him. An answer that eventually made its way into the holy book of Muslims, the Quran (also spelled Koran, and Qur'an): Remember, he responded when questioned as to who the God of Islam was by saying; "He is God the One God, the eternal. He begot no one nor was He begotten. No one is comparable to Him (112:1-4). He is to be worshiped as the only God."

What is so disconcerting about that information is the fact that Islam has already indicated they will use nuclear force to make people understand that Allah will prevail in eliminating the Creator God. That is what they say. And their literature seems to verify that as a fact. Most who study Islam, and many Christians who have not studied Islam, seem to agree that it was for that very reason—to eliminate Christ, or at least abolish Him, thus removing Him from this earth, that Allah was brought into existence. How much sway will Islam have in the future? That is unknown. But prior to Covid, their involvement, as was being preached, put them front and center in many of the last day scenarios. Some were even saying they would probably be involved in bring about the battle of Armageddon.

Let me ask a question, and it is not a rhetorical question: Is that not the desires of Satan dating as far back as when he was known as Lucifer, when he rebelled against God, taking a third of the angels with him, and, declaring that one day he would overthrow God? And what better way than to battle His Son, Jesus Christ, here on earth, thus abolishing both God and His Son? That is, if Satan were to be victorious. A battle fought by the surrogate of Satan, known as the antichrist. A battle of good versus evil. A battle that most can see coming. Most say, it appears to be a battle for all the marbles. And since a Christian knows how everything turns out, one could say, it is for all the marbles, and Satan loses.

A battle that will culminate with the coming of Christ, and the fulfillment of future biblical prophecy that says Christ will be victorious, and we, as His followers, will be victorious as well. Having said that, it appears that would put Muslims on the other side of the fence with the coming of Christ, but they contend it will be their messiah that will be coming. And remember, he will be coming; "With Jesus as his personal executioner."

To arrive at that point, they will use every resource available, many we have already seen. Remember, when it was said, that Muslims (Islam) will live in peace while biding their time until they can conquer their opponents—opponents being infidels, such as friends, co-works, neighbors, doesn't matter, when Allah comes calling, all will answer. They continue to say that one day, the Islamic Messiah will sit as lord in Jerusalem. And how committed they are to accomplishing that for Allah? Well, considering it is a destiny given to them by Allah, they take the words very seriously.

Remember earlier when John Hagee told us that they must destroy Israel OR, Allah would be perceived as a false god, and Muhammad would be considered a false prophet? How many think that will ever happen? Right. But the dilemma for Muslims to prove Islam to be a true religion, and Allah to be conceived as a God, Islam must destroy all who serve a different God, and tax the heck out of those who will not subjugate themselves to Islamic beliefs. And for all of this to occur, as Islamic literature dictates, total victory for Allah must be achieved. But as we find out. there are obstacles in their way.

Try as they must to remove the Jews from their promised land, that won't happen. If for no other reason than Israel won't let that happen, if for no other reason than what has been referred to as the "Samson Option." They will only induce violence if they feel threatened. Well, most ask," are they not threatened almost daily from at least one or more of their neighbors?" They realize it is the destiny of Islam to destroy them, to push them into the sea.

As Muslims continue the course they are on, and with Israel keeping a sharp eye on them, the question might become, when will one, or the other, feel they must act, and act immediately for self-preservation? That may not happen tomorrow, but common sense says it is going to happen. Will the world be brought into a war against itself? Everyone knows if this happens, it would probably be the end of civilization, at least civilization as we know it.

For those who may not know, Israel has more than 126 nuclear bombs they will use in their defense. When it comes to the destruction of Israel, I don't think anyone expects the people of Israel to just lie down when their very survival is at stake as they still have memories of the Holocaust. The Sampson Option is a nuclear option available to Israel and will be invoked when and if they feel all options for future survival have been exhausted. For more information regarding the Samson Option, read Seymour M. Hersh's book *The Sampson Option*.

For the moment, let's go behind a smidgin of the history that has evolved into the Islam most Muslims follow today. And most of that is centered around the Islam that was embraced during the early years of expansion. What many find surprising, is knowing what we know about the Islamic religion, and yet, many still assist them in establishing themselves into the very fiber of our society, and with American citizens money. How crazy is that? Only in America.

I'm talking about the number of Mosques that we have built for them in America and abroad. With that in mind, it might be interesting to observe what takes place in the halls of worship for Islam. For the moment, let us look at some of the events that bring about the current day's activities. Activities toward humanity as has been perpetrated by Muslims upon Jews and Christians. Activities that have spilled over onto the rest of the world. Activities that are discussed quite regularly in many of the Islamic worship centers throughout the country, commonly referred to as a "Mosque."

Islamic worship centers

With the continuing influx of Muslims, the trend of building mosques continues. Some states have been known to help Muslims build these worship centers, as well as paying for them to be built abroad. Yep, America is helping to build mosques in the Middle East in the effort of building relationships. Who would be against building a place of worship to establish friendships? Again, all in the interest of saying "hey, we're not so bad." But it may just be because we appear to exude the mentality of believing, "Hey, look at us, we don't understand what we're doing, but we want to do it better than anyone else." Of course, I jest, but sometimes it feels that way.

When one thinks about Islam and the religion associated with Islam, why would any country build Muslims worship centers to worship an alien god, at least alien to a Judeo-Christian nation. If you have not paid much attention, as most might not, you would not likely be aware of the propaganda and preaching of hate toward infidels emulating from many of these mosques. There is anti-American, anti-Israel, as well as pro-conquest, and pro-expansion, kind of preaching that can be heard. Unlike places of worship that preach a different God, such as, churches, synagogues, and temples. Mosques, according to Erick Stakelbeck, are embraced as recruitment centers, as well as for transferring of arms and cash, and back-door meetings, while praying to Allah in the main worship center.

Mosques are being built within America, and are being financed by Saudi money, with state subsidies in several states. Think about that for a moment. Would that not give the Muslim

Brotherhood, and the Brotherhood of Islam, sworn enemies of America, enemies who want to rip our heads from our bodies, a foothold on American soil? An extraordinarily strong foothold. Also, did you notice how Saudi money is building mosques over here and we are helping to finance mosques over there? Although this was some time back the sentiment has not changed.

Another demand upon a Muslim is regular attendance at a Mosque and praying to Allah five times a day. Speaking of Mosque, Muslims consider them a place that serves to settle disputes, discuss charitable causes, exchange information, and educate the un-believer. As Muhammad said, "Whoever goes to the mosque in the morning and evening, Allah will prepare for him an honorable place in the Paradise every time he goes and comes."

Attending a mosque is encouraged as it promotes socializing with other Muslims, and in exchange, brings them closer to each other and makes the society stronger. Many activities go on in mosques that one might find in a Christian church, asking forgiveness for sins happens to be one. Let us see. Are there others? Nope. That is all that come to mind. As for the rest, praying to be right with Allah, praying for Allah's will to be done, and so on, is the primary function of a Mosque. Much of what one might find in a Protestant church they might find in a mosque, only the spiritual entity is Allah, rather than Jesus.

Apart from being a place for congregational prayers and other collective worship practices, a mosque, likewise, furnishes Muslims with other most vital social amenities as well. Mosques serve as the seat of the Prophet Muhammad's government, a learning center, a hospital, a rehabilitation center, a welfare center, and the place for legitimate recreational actives. Within the Muslim community, as mentioned earlier, great comradery is found. It was also brought to our attention earlier that it is more the religion embraced by the people rather than the people. But the people become dangerous because of the religion they embrace. You see the paradox that Hank Hanegraaff brought to our attention earlier? Muslim Iman's within these mosques content that the mosque is where the heart of Islam resides. A place where one will hear preached, the purpose of human creation, is to worship Allah. And be thankful to Him, for what he has bestowed upon them as his chosen. They honestly believe they are the chosen, as much as does a Christian. Thanking Allah for their daily life is simply a way towards worshipping the exalted god.

As they say, whatever we are today, and we do today, is because of his favors. I guess one could say that about a Christian, and the Christian God. In the Holy Quran Allah says: "O you, who have believed, eat from the good things which we have provide for you and be grateful to Allah if it is Him that you worship?" (Quran, 2:172).

From the Hadith we come to know that every single word of recitation from the Quran helps to understand the words of Allah with great daily rewards. In fact, whoever reads a letter of the book of Allah, followed by a good deed, gets tenfold reward. I am not exactly sure what that means. But Muslims are told that by reciting the Quran daily, it helps Muslims in understanding the words of Allah. Same with a Christian and the Bible. I guess the rewards being a better life now, and eternal life later, both sound like good rewards to me.

While over the years, various mosques have been built in America with Middle Eastern money, some in many cases, have been subsidized with American money, if not outright paid for— with American money. For those not paying much attention, the number of mosques in the United States quietly rose from 1,290 in 2000 to 2,106 in 2010. Not bad, eight hundred and sixteen in ten years. Not bad compared to the later years.

It has been estimated there were somewhere around one hundred mosques in the U.S. in 1970, but the immigration of several million Muslims, probably more like tens of millions since then, has led to a couple thousand more mosques being built with the possibility of many more on the planning board, as the world embraces for the impact from the latest immigration crisis. A poll conducted in 2011 found that the number of mosques to be 2,106 and then the 2020 version found 2,769 mosques—more than double the number from only a decade earlier.[46]

I really thought America knew Muslims and the religion they serve better than what we have witnessed. They have been telling us how they feel and what they want to do to us, all of us, as infidels, and have for many years. And yet, we elect them to serve in our sacred halls of liberty. With this lack of understanding, how is America to survive? Wherever they get a majority they will continue changing governments. And according to the last count, approximately two hundred Muslims, dedicated to Allah, will be running for governmental positions in 2020. One could say it was during that period, the gates of democracy were opened for future Muslims to breach the halls of Justice.

Anyway, it appears that currently, we are setting ourselves up for having refugee problems. Refugees that are migrating to America to seek a better life, I know that is debatable, but times are different now. A few years ago, migrants who were dangerous to America, were infiltrating our country with extraordinarily little notice. Refugees and migrants, some good, some bad, were crossing our boarder unhindered by law. But things have changed as we are about to see.

After several years of our government protecting our borders, protecting American citizens, America is once again uninterested in who is entering our country. That is obvious by the lack of interest our government is investing in knowing who is coming in. And that would include granting access to dangerous individuals with very little notice, even helping them in some situations.

---

[46] https://www.pewresearch.org

Wait! What? Say that again! If I understand what was just said, I find, a lot has changed, and yet, the more it changes, the more it appears the same. A question we might be asking ourselves, how many of those entering our country may desire to bring tragedy to America and its citizens? I do not believe anyone can answer that question with any accuracy, but looking back over some material I had saved, I came across information that might give us an idea. Material that is outdated, but implies we were oblivious to the threat then, almost twenty years ago, as we are now.

The potential number of those entering our country illegally at one time, could be summed up in an editorial article written by Stuart Anderson, Executive Director of the National Foundation for American Policy published in Time magazine October 25, 2004. He was quoting an earlier published article. The article he was quoting asserted that 190,000 non-Mexican undocumented immigrants—including those who came from terrorist hot spots—and settled here in the year 2004.

Current times. Since our border patrol is currently not retaining individuals from these hot spots, just as they were not retaining them then, those who wish to do us harm, appear to be entering our country unimpeded once again. Can anyone refute that statement? The more, up-to-date information that is available, seems to be telling us that approximately 200,000 illegals are entering our country every month.

Every month. Wow! I must repeat that, "every single month," approximately 200,000 unvetted individuals are entering our country. Does one think that there will not be any repercussions from the open boarders of America? And, at last count, they could be settling in New York, Washington, Ohio, Virginia, Florida, throughout Oregon, California and Texas just waiting for the command from Allah to bring about more destruction, if not here, then somewhere in the world.

The last I heard from Dave Robbins of End-Time's ministry was, "There are 430,000 operatives in over thirty countries, and it would be naïve to think that some are not living in the U.S." When Dave mentioned "Operatives," many would categorize that word as meaning, the "Merciless Avengers," those cold-blooded killers, we discussed earlier. Those that are positioned around the world just waiting for the signal from Allah.

And when they hear that word, they turn into Syed Farook and his wife, Tashfeen Malik. Remember when they heard Allah calling? They shot those who threw them a baby shower, just days earlier. They live among us in numbers that continue to grow daily. But again, as Nancy Pelosi said about the Affordable Health Care Bill, (Obama Care), "we will have to wait to see what's in it." As for Muslims, as well as all who are entering our country, I guess we will have to wait to see how things turn out. This is in addition to a government prone to making decisions that are quite questionable when it comes to the safety of America and its citizens.

XXII

The Terrorist Next Door

WITH THE CONTINUING INFLUX OF Muslims, the trend of building mosques continues. Some states are even helping Muslims build mosques as well as paying for them to be built abroad in an effort to build relationships. After all, who would be against building a place of worship to establish friendships. Again, all in the interest of saying "hey, we're not so bad." But it probably is more like saying "hey, look at us, we don't understand what we're doing" but we want to do it better than anyone else. At least, that is probably how Islam views us. I don't believe that it is only Islam looking at us that way, many Americans are beginning to adopt that attitude as well.

Speaking of mosque as we were a moment ago, if you want to learn more about what goes on inside a mosque read Erick Stakelbeck's book, *The Terrorist Next Door*. Erick's book discusses the dangers of Islam and tells us about what goes on inside of mosques, mosques for the most part, that are being welcomed in many states. Only in America would it be allowed to erect a place of worship by an enemy that is diabolical opposed to the God the country was built upon—the creator God—while plotting how to eliminate him, and everyone associated with him. Again, only in America. Erick also has written a very good book titled, *The Muslim Brotherhood*. Given the amount of reality that is contained in that book, it's a book that will curl your toes.

Probably what disturbs most about some of the mosques being built is the fact that many Muslim organizations are even receiving help from the citizens by way of tax breaks and other incentives to erect shrines to Allah just to fulfill our obligation of giving religious freedom to everyone. That is what a lot of this is about, giving religious freedom to those who want to do us harm in the name of their religion? And, if they run into any opposition, they have the ACLU right there to help them. Help them sometimes in ways that are not beneficial to America but based upon defending political correction. And in some cases, they aid in the destruction to America. Political correction is such a b**** sometimes.

Also, there are those American citizens who seem to go out of their way to help Muslims any way they can in hopes of projecting the image of, "Hey we're pretty good people." Which might be followed by the Democrats saying, "remember to vote for us." I was about to say only in America again, but it appears to be happening in Europe and throughout other parts of the world as well.

Mosques that are being built within America, and as we saw, many being financed by Saudi money. Think about that for a moment, that gives the Muslim Brotherhood, and the Brotherhood of Islam, sworn enemies of America, enemies who want to rip our heads from our bodies, a foothold on American soil. A very strong foothold. Also, did you notice how Saudi money is building mosques over here and we are financing mosques over there? A strange world in which we live

Fight in the name of Allah

Allah is great, Allah is good, Allah is God, Allah must be worshiped. Every Muslim, without exception, is committed to the *shahada*— "There is no god but Allah, and Muhammad is the Messenger of Allah." Love of the Prophet runs like blood in the veins of the Muslim community. One may deny Allah, but it is impossible to deny Muhammad. He is venerated as the Truth, the Exalted, the Forgiver, the Raiser of the Dead, the Chosen of

God, the Seal of the prophets, the Mediator, the Shining Star, the Justifier, and the perfect one."[47] Then we have Zafeera Siddique who declares Islam is not just a religion but a way of life, the only way of life.

As mentioned before, considering the conditions as set forth by Islam many find it incompatible with the Judeo-Christian values of Christianity. The condition that sets the tone for everyone to coexist and find peace with Muslims is found in the Quran (the Muslim Bible, the Recitation, meaning readings and narrations). Also, information for how to coexist is included within sacred Muslim text, the Hadiths—notes depicting the actions and teachings as recorded by Muhammad and his followers. The Hadith is an accumulation of authoritative sayings and actions of Muhammad, and the opinions of legal scholars.

The Hadiths along with the Quran resulted in the formation of Sharia law—laws Muslims believe to have been spoken by God himself to Muhammad. As we saw earlier, Sharia law is insane but since it was spoken by Allah it will endure for as long as Allah endures. Since Muslims believe the instructions came from Allah himself, they feel compelled to obey them. To disobey would equate to a Christian rejecting, or at least mitigating Christ. For example, the five daily prayers are obligatory upon Muslims. Those who do not perform them are committing a sin, and they will be held accountable for that on the day of judgment.

Anyway, as we were discussing, there are conditions imposed upon us (infidels) to cohabitate with Muslims. These terms and conditions are set forth by the Quran. If your neighbor or co-worker is a Muslim and he follows Muhammad and bows to Allah, he probably subscribes to the following. The next time you see a Muslim praying, the following might be a good example of what he might be reciting from the Quran.

---

[47] Hanegraaff, Hank. *Muslim.*

Fight those who do not believe in Allah, nor in
the latter day, nor do they prohibit what Allah
and His Apostle have prohibited, nor follow the
religion of truth out of those who have been
given the Book, until they pay the Jizya [tax] in
acknowledgment of superiority and they are in a
state of subjection."[48] Or as Islam says, "until they
pay the *Jizya* with willing submission, and feel
themselves subdued." (Q 9:29).

State of subjection! Wow! State of subjection and willing
submission. Once again, is revealing that information about Islam
being Islamophobic, maybe even racist? I mention John Hagee
and reference his book *"Jerusalem Countdown"* as he tells us the
destiny of Islam is to defeat Israel, wiping the name of Israel and
the God of Israel from the history books. We are just standing
in the way and slated for elimination. If Israel goes then reason
would dictate that Christians must also go. We all know this
has been the goal/destiny of Islam for generations, but again the
question is why? The answer is Hate, godless hate. Hate directed
by the "angel of light" upon the world whereas Christianity is
directed by the light of Christ. Again, two separate entities.

We saw where the Quran discussed our demise at the hands
of Islam, now let's see what the Hadith has to say about our future:

"Fight in the name of Allah and in the way of
Allah. Fight against those who disbelieve in Allah.
[The infidels of the world.] Make a holy war...
When you meet your enemies who are polytheist
[Christians are polytheist as they believe in a
Trinity] invite them to three courses of action. If

---

[48] William J. Bennett and Seth Leibsohn. *The Fight of Our Lives: Knowing
the Enemy, Speaking the Truth & Choosing to Win the War Against Radical
Islam.* Thomas Nelson. 2011.

they respond to any one of these, you also accept it and withhold yourself from doing them any harm. Invite them to Islam; if they respond to you, accept it from them and desist from fighting against them...If they refuse to accept Islam, demand from them the Jizya [the subjugation tax]. If they agree to pay, accept it from them and hold off your hands. If they refuse to pay the tax, seek Allah's help, and fight them.[49]

Which as we have seen is interpreted as "cutting off their heads, slitting their throats, drowning them, or burning them to death for not either converting or paying a subjugation tax." Wow! Sounds as if paying a tax assures protection from death. I must tell you none of that sounds very appealing to anyone. One thing I do know is that understanding true Christianity places a target on the back of a Christian, if for no other reason than their believe in the Trinity—Father, Son, and Holy Spirit.

Because of this believe we are considered as being a polytheistic religion, a religious belief that acts as pollution to the world of Islam. Islam declares Christians who believe in the Trinity to be guilty of *shirk*. Which equates to "associating something with God." (Idol worship in Christianity). This is considered the most heinous sin in Islam and another reason to rid the world of Christians. And that is to remove this tainted blood from the world.

Muslims say the tainted blood of infidels will never be mingled with the purity of Islam blood. This has justified many honor killings. Again, there doesn't seem to be any way of holding that tiger back as those instructions come from Allah himself as conveyed to the world by Muhammad. When considering

---

[49] Erick Stakelbeck *The Terrorist Next Door--How the Government is Deceiving you about the Islamist Threat*. Regnery Publishing, Inc. 2011.

the destiny of Islam, again one might consider the words of Jay Sekulow as he tells us; "Islam teaches that the blood of infidels is not equal to the blood of Muslims and commands them to treat non-Muslims harshly and fellow Muslims mercifully." Wow! Nothing convoluted about those words.

Factual Reality

Considering this command of obedience towards Muhammad and Allah, logic dictates we accept two facts: One, a non-Muslim will never be equal to a Muslim because of tainted blood. Muslims are too committed and dedicated in the ideology of their beliefs to accept non-Muslims as equal. If they do, they are not following, verbatim, the directions of the Quran, or the prophet Muhammad, or more importantly, Allah, and for this an eternity in hell may await them.

And two, we need to embrace the fact that we are infidels worthy only of death. And as such, we are considered less than human, more like cattle to be slaughtered in sacrifice to Allah. I actually read that in Islamic literature. If that be the situation, then America seems to discount the severity of the problem with Islam, and that would indicate we may have already lost our way as a country. Especially when the destiny of Islam is added into the fray of other things that are currently happening in our lives.

Think about that, we currently have serving in our government, those of Islamic descend, along with Muslim sympathizers who are very prevalent in the decision making for America, otherwise, we would not have given billions of dollars of weapons and technology to our enemy. We would not have left hundreds of Americans to die at the hands of our enemies. And we would not be inviting them to dinner.

As I was typing that I got to thinking about the Muslims who have been elected to serve in our government. They appear to be nice Muslims who dislike those who stand with Israel; they appear to be for America, that is if America stands with the Palestinians; they appear to be for using problems facing Americans to fuel the flames of hate within our country. A great ploy of Islam is to push their agenda upon a divided country fighting itself. The more displeasure and disruption they cause Americans, the happier they are as that is what they are striving to achieve. Divide and conquer. And yet we invite them into our country. Go figure.

An area of contention for many Americans is the swearing in of Muslims on the Quran rather than the Bible. The latest one I am familiar with was Solicitor General of Michigan, Fadwa Hammoud who was sworn into office on the Quran. And we as a Judeo-Christian country accept that. If I'm not mistaken, the Bible talks about the moments we seem to be witnessing. Calling evil good and good evil. Moments that are brought to us from the book of Revelation. So the coming days should not come as any surprise to a Christian.

With Islam we are dealing with deception on an extensive scale. We know deception exist within Islam and appears to be a staple within that religion. Within the very core of Islamic ideology deception exists. God was removed and substituted with another god, (idol) to worship, as it is not the God who gave life, wrote Geneses, and concluded with Revelation.

I would put Muslims who follow Allah, beside those who embrace theology that says, "whatever the means followed that justifies our end is okey to pursue." Meaning Muslims, not only Muslims, but prosperity preachers as well, seem to feel they are justified in lying, cheating, manipulating or using any form of deception to further their ambitions. With the prosperity preachers they need to raise money for that multi-million-dollar plane, but for the Muslims, ethnic cleansing, domination, and control are foremost requirements within their religion. And when it comes to accomplishing their destiny, anything is fair in love and war.

Those who worship Allah as a God and have vowed to follow only him, thus, disavowing the God our country was founded upon. As well as helping to build mosques that furthers their agenda in their quest to bring Islam to America. We encourage our schools to teach Islam as a good thing, and how by respecting Allah and Muslims, we are better citizens. Only in America. At the end of this book is a letter from an ex-Muslim that will set the tone for what you are about to read. If you would like to take a moment and read it. You might not believe what you are reading but it reveals the depth of deception that exist within Islam.

XXIII

The Deception of Islam

I REALIZE IT IS POLITICALLY incorrect, as well as offense to the Islamic community, to discuss the possibility that deception might exist within Islam, but that would be denying the factual evidence that has already been presented as well as more evidence that will be presented later. Evidence describing in some detail how Islam, through deception, will one day crown Allah as the king of this world. The only way I can emphasize the deception that exists within Islam is to say that if we looked in the dictionary under "deception" we would probably be instructed to "see Islam." Also, as mentioned, within the Muslim vocabulary the words Quraysh and Taqiyya can be found meaning patience and deception respectfully.

Living in a Judeo-Christian country one would not expect to find the word Taqiyya—meaning "deceitful" along with Quraysh which means to deceive by deception as well, but a "revengeful" kind of deception. Although, while deception is deception, the depth of the word deception has different meanings. Deception, a very large animal in the current world and one that is being embraced by Islam, and let me also throw in Secularist, Humanist, and New Ager's as they denounce the existence of a God. Islam might denounce our God, but the current generation denounces any God.

Does anyone think Muslims who embrace Muhammad's teachings about the Islamic god will stop any time soon and denounce fourteen hundred years of Muslim history? Not a chance. Not and be faithful to Allah, and therein lies the problem (rub) for the world going forward. Especially America. As a country founded upon Judeo-Christian values, and considered the last bastille of Christian beliefs, it will be targeted to endure more horrendous scenes like 9/11. Perhaps that is why we are turning more from God and more to appeasement. Perhaps we are satisfied with appeasement, as it brings peace from Islam for the moment, but Islam cannot cohabitate with anyone, or any country, who does not bow to Allah. That is evidenced by their literature where it says we will serve Allah, and no other God, or we will acknowledge his Superiority by paying a severe penalty, and if anyone refuses to pay what Islam calls a subjugation tax, they will be put to death as a sacrifice to Allah. Just saying, you will recognize the Superiority of Allah, or you will die. And that is a promise.

The Islamic code should be, "no matter how long it takes to get there, have patience and we will overcome." But now that Iran is approaching the place in history where they are going to be acquiring a nuclear bomb or two, and have promised to use them, the goal posts have been moved considerable closer to those times the book of Revelation keeps referring to.

Anyway, the problem with deception is determining how to know its deception, especially if it is coming from someone we trust. For example, if I told you we need to make friends with all people, including those who follow Islam, and intensify our dialogue with them as well as nonbelievers, and extend an olive branch of peace to them, would you agree? Probably. Extending an olive branch in the name of peace seems like an honorable thing to do.

Again, not much imagination is needed to comprehend that extending an olive branch in the name of peace is good for the whole world. The alternative to coexist with Muslims, as we've seen, is to be subject to Islam, so any attempt to live in peace that excludes the subjection part of their religion is welcome. But if that is not possible, the question that must be asked then might be, "whom are we extending this olive branch to in the interest of peace?" If I said it would be okay to extend that olive branch to people who believe that Christ is not the Son of God, (strike one) but that he is only a prophet who has now become a Muslim (strike two) and works for the Islamic messiah, al Mahdi in bringing about the total extermination of infidels (strike three) would you still want to intensify communication and extend an olive branch?

Probably some would, as we seem to witness from time to time. If not, we wouldn't be so eager to invite them to dinner. It would probably be safe to say that most if not all liberals would vote for appeasement, and that means acceptance, and that means kicking the can down the road. But it seems to be nobody's fault as the Bible alludes to these times as "must occur times." Christians know what that means and stand ready to take the future on—as Charles Stanley says, with Christ. And the Bible tells us, "All things are possible." This may not be a big issue to a Secularist or a Humanist, as they embrace the religion of atheism, or agnosticism, or New Ageism, and bow more to the god of "self-wisdom." But to accept a god other than the Living God, and I say living, because the others are still dead, is unacceptable deception within the ranks of the Christian community.

A foothold or beachhead has been achieved in America and with that foothold they will continue to advance their cause through their Iman's who, preach the lordship of Allah. They preach to do the will of Allah and he will reward you and he will love you and he will bring you more peace by bringing adversity to the infidels, always follow the guidance of Allah. Continue following the teachings as brought forth by the Iman's, and Allah will give your life meaning, and so on.

Many have concluded from following the destiny of Islam that a lot of the planning for those moments of violence and conquest is disseminated through the various mosque that can be found almost anywhere in America. With the information covered so far would that not be considered sitting ourselves up to be manipulated by those who have said over and over, they want to remove us by any means possible, and plant an Islamic flag over our Capital?

They embrace the ideology that says, "if the means justifies the end," then Allah promotes the concept of "go for it." Especially if the means promotes an end that promotes Islam. Meaning Muslims are justified in bringing the world into the Islamic faith, even if it might seem insane, immoral, inhumane, coldblooded, and yes, even a little sadistic to the outside world. But, if it brings the world closer to recognizing Allah as the only god, and furthers the cause of removing the Living God, then go for it. Every Christian knows how that would turn out.

But for now, one finds lurking under the surface of the façade of Islam unpresented evil. I am thinking of ISIS as a true representation of Islam who, not long ago, destroyed everything in their path, including humans, when the opportunity to expand Islam presented itself. The core of Islam was demonstrated and put on display for the world to see during that period. They have, at least for the moment, been stopped from spreading genocide, but Islam is never "truly" stopped.

Someday, especially if backed by the right allies, they may not be stopped. At least that is what fourteen hundred years of history conveys to us. It appears that the world is searching for peace, even Muslims say they are advocates of peace. With that in mind, there is a new word that has been embraced by some searching for a diplomatic solution to ending the conflict between Muslims and Christians. You might find the next sub-section interesting if you follow the logic as to why some think Chrislam might work while others say no way. What some think might work, is found to be impossible by others. See what you think.

The deception of Chrislam

In addition to Taqiyya and Quraysh, probably the most deceptive word that seems to be floating around the halls of Christendom lately and has been for a while is "Chrislam." Considering the meaning of that word, how can a Christian even consider the deception attached to it. Chrislam is the merging or coming together as one, the religion of Christianity and the religion of Islam. If one understood that each have different agendas, agendas that include promoting God's that are diabolically opposed to each other, how then can anything, other than appeasement exist?

There would always be a separation as we worship different God's. But the primary difference between these two God's and the people who follow them is the fact that one would have no problem ripping our head from our body for not accepting the God of Islam. That fear will always be there. We know this to be true, otherwise we would be at peace and would go to the same mosque or church to praise Allah or Christ? Do we worship and accept Allah, or do we worship the Creator God? Do we worship Christ, or do we fall under the control of al Mahdi? Since Rick Warren as well as the Catholic church thinks Chrislam might work, I wonder how they would answer those questions, being a Christian and all.

In the Bible Christ is portrayed as the savior of the world, the Son of God, while in Islam, Christ is portrayed as a merciless avenger working for the Islamic Messiah eliminating non-converts for al Mahdi. How does one square that thinking with Chrislam? The intent behind Chrislam may be motivated by the interest of searching for a degree of peace, any peace, as that would hopefully negate the problems plaguing the world and bring with it a bit of heavenly bliss in the form of some quality time from a world that seemingly has gone mad. But chaos must come, or Islam is not advancing the cause they were put on this earth to fulfill. It is their destiny to eliminate the God of the Jews and in so doing they eliminate Christians and Christianity. You say it can't happen, perhaps not, but that won't keep them from trying.

Anyway, in the interest of peace, we watch the evolution of Chrislam. But for now, the advancement of Chrislam has been slowed for obvious reasons. Charles Kimball tells us in his book *When Religions Become Evil* that the conflicts the world is encountering are being inflected by Islamic extremist and is out of the norm of Islam. Really? Is he telling us we don't understand Islam, or is he saying that if we understood Islam, we would know how peaceful it is? Is that what he is saying? In other words, what we witness as facts, and what Islam presents with words, doesn't represent Islam and would be considered "out of the norm?" Is that what he is saying?

He says, "It is both contradictory to the spirit of Islam and highly counterproductive. Muslims committed to peaceful coexistence and constructive change through nonviolent means must step forward and provide leadership that truly reflects their affirmation that Islam is a religion of peace." Standing up or not, that would only promulgate more deception as there isn't a Muslim who could in all good conscience say Islam is a nonaggressive religion without being deceptive.

It would be nice to be convinced that Islam is a passive religion, considering the violence witnessed by Islam over the years. Peace from Islam probably fits under the category of wishful thinking. Besides, any Muslim who could come forth and tout the virtues of, "Islam being committed to peaceful constructive change through non-violent means," would be considered by many to be an illusionist. How can anyone tout the virtues of Islam considering the core of Islam is one of dominance and subversion. Remember, convert, pay a tax, or die. They never have said, "or you "may" die. They don't mince many words when they said, "you will die." Words straight from Allah to Muhammad and presented as gospel in the Qur'an.

Richard Bennett

The Qur'an

The Quran: What is the Quran anyway? We know it to be a set of writings and interpretations from the Islamic Prophet Muhammad, and we know it to be holy in the sight of a Muslim but how might a Christian decipher the same information from the same book? Let's listen in to a couple of experts as they answer that question. First from Hank Hanegraaff as he says, "The Qur'an is clearly an unreliable revelation. It prostitutes the Bible, denies the deity of Christ, misrepresents the Trinity, repudiates the cross, and more. It is replete with faulty ethics, riddled with factual errors, and its eloquence is but feigned." Then we hear from Samuel Zwemer, a longtime Christian missionary in Arabia as he says:

> Islam thrives only by its denial of the authority of the Scriptures, the deity of our Lord, the blessedness of the Holy Trinity, the cruciality and significance of the cross and the preeminence of Jesus Christ as King and Savior. And this great denial by the assertion of the authority of another book, the Koran, the eclipse of Christ's glory by another prophet, even Muhammad, and the substitution of another path to forgiveness and holiness for the way of the cross. The denials and assertions are imbedded in the Koran and are the orthodox belief of all who know anything of their religion.

I do not believe it is possible to disavow anything more vehemently than what was just said and yet, many believe the Bible and the Quran contain basically the same information as you are about to see. One more. Martin Luther writing at a crucial juncture during the long and torturous struggle between Islam and Europe described Muhammad's Qur'an as "a foul and shameful book."[50] The law of Allah, said Luther, is tantamount to the law of the sword. He also said:

> It is commanded in their law, as a good and divine work, that they shall rob and murder, devour and destroy more and more those that are round about them, and they do this, and think that they are doing God service.[51]

I'm with Luther on this one. They think they are doing the will of the Creator God by doing the bidding of Allah. Luther continues:

> Their government, (the Islamic religion) therefore, is not a regular rulership, like others for the maintenance of peace, the protection of the good, and the punishment of the wicked, but a rod of anger and a punishment of God (Allah) upon the unbelieving world.[52]

Again, a religion that doesn't seem to fit into the structure of the world. Anyway, nothing said will ever deter a Muslim from following Muhammad. As they say, a Muslim is a Muslim, is a Muslim. A person with a strong commitment to Allah and the Quran. But then, perhaps that is to be commended. I found that same commitment present when the reformers, many of whom were asked to die for their convictions, did so willingly rather than retract one word they found to be true. They may have watched as wood was being stacked around them with a torch nearby, but they never repudiated their faith in the Christian God.

---

[50] Hank Hanegraaff. *Muslim*. West Publishing Group. Nashville, Tenn. 2017.

[51] Ibid

[52] Ibid

It's not hard to find the differences between Islam and the rest of the world. One dies rationalizing a religion—justifying, as well as vindicating killings and destruction to achieve their goal, while the other dies confirming—endorsing, as well as sanctioning a religion of meaning, of substance, of love and peace. I guess what it all comes down to, what seems to be bottom line; Muslims are betting on their guy while Christians are betting on theirs.

XXIV

The Dilemma of Peace

IT SEEMS TO MANY THAT peace and love go together. Without one we cannot have the other. Peace in the Middle East seems to be a dilemma that many have tried to solve over the centuries by producing peace treaties, peace accords, and peace agreements by the dozens and have accomplished very little in the way of reconciling the two sides. Conflicts continue over land, religion, ideology, and even the right to exist. Conflicts have plagued the Middle East for some time with discontent and chaos. With each giving rise to the thinking; maybe there's a reason for current activities to be occurring as they are.

Bringing peace to the Middle East has been the goal of every president dating back to, well as far back as I can remember. Since the 1970's when Yasser Arafat was the Islamic leader for the Islamic nation, and probably many years before that. There has been a parallel effort made to find terms upon which peace can be agreed upon for decades, and yet, peace is still allusive. Many attempts have resulted in both the Arab-Israel conflict and the Palestinian-Israeli conflict being settled. By settled, I mean Israel giving up land, the Gaza Strip, from which now Islam is lobbing bombs into Israel, and have since day one of occupying the strip. That includes the West Bank and the trouble with Muslims and Jews disagreeing as to who should be there.

While Islam continues to harass Israel and its citizens America seems to be in the crosshairs of Islam. Even to the extent of constantly being harass by those who have chosen to drive cars or trucks into pedestrians or blow up a couple of buildings or create explosions that cause panic such as the Boston marathon bombing, as well as downing a plane or two. In other words, no agreement will bring peace except for the seven-year peace agreement arranged by the antichrist, so says the Bible.

There are events that grab our attention from time to time as we are aware. Events that can have an overreach into our peace of mind, events such as wars, and rumors of wars, skirmishes and conflicts that seem to escalate from time to time and slice through our minds with everlasting concerns. And that would include terrorism, the whack-a-mole kind of terrorism former President Obama spoke about. The kind of terrorism that seems to be brought to us by Islam and those who follow Islam which is designed to leave a state of paranoia and intimidation wherever the religion of Islam goes.

Those are words that a Muslim does not want to hear and words that will put me in the same corner as Joel Richardson, but did he lie? Am I lying? And again, am I, or the thousands who study Islam lying in exposing Islam for what it really is, a religion or movement that is hell bent on conquest at any cost. But we know that.

And for those who say we should just leave the Muslims alone as they are not invading our space right now. And they finish with, why publish a book of this nature? A book that seems to be filled with animosity towards a group of people, and according to many, that is racist. And since that group of raciest infidels are identified as anti-Islamic by Muslims, they would be slated to die as prescribed by Allah. And carried out, as we have seen, by Muslims in the war against infidels. And anyone who discusses the differences of the religions are Islamophobic. Is that what is being said?

Even though their goals, and as has been mentioned a time or two, even their destiny, is the demise of America and Israel, along with Canada, Europe and others. Without an understand of that, if we don't recognize what was just said, and see the picture, the complete picture, then maybe even prayer for America is behind us. The picture being discussed is the same picture Joel Richardson, Hal Lindsey and John Hagee sees, along with many others such as Patrick Herron, Jack Van Impe and a new name, Michael Youssef, executive president of *Leading the Way,* and others who are speaking out to the dangers of Islam.

Because of the description the Bible portrays of things to come, we are going to have other events that disrupt our peace of mind from time to time. Including, but not limited to, some home-grown atrocities such as stabbings, shooting, property damage, and disrespect towards our law enforcement officials, from dousing them with water to killing them. Granted, those actions were perpetrated by non-Muslims, but they were just as equal in the level of hate that accompanies the actions of Islam.

Now, we are talking about the kind of hate that affects the mind. Hate that is manifested by the bombings we endure from time to time, as well as the attempted bombings, along with school shootings, mall shootings, shootings in general, and hate from twisted minds that can be found within the very fabric of America as brought to us by such gangs as MS13. Who can believe we have currently in America, those who would have no problem peeling off our face and sewing it to a basketball? And with an "open boarder" policy, who's to say how many members of the MS13 gang have come to America.

Hate witnessed from time-to-time causing fear, anger, concern, and frustration. All ingredients associated with last day theology. Even to the extent of blaming inanimate objects (guns) for killing people. The more disruption witnessed in America, the more the left will go after guns when the gun is not to blame No, it is people killing people using inanimate object to accomplish such atrocities. Sometimes it's as if we are living in an institution that appears to be going crazier with each passing year. Each passing year? Now it seems almost with each passing monthly. Exactly the description of the times before we are told it really gets rough.

While the world is rising to becoming a boiling point of hostility, it's interesting to watch the news when they try to dissect the problems. News that is brought to us by individuals who themselves are searching for the meaning of things. I can't be the only one who sometimes feels as if I'm watching the blind leading the blind. Leaders without a clue, journalist who seem to be rearranging the deck chairs on the titanic, and so on. Politicians who are not business orientated and lack the knowledge of leadership when it comes to running a country. Islam knows this and plays us like a violin. And it is the thinking of Islam, associating us with an apathic nation, that will continue affecting our peace of mind and disrupting our ability to live in peace.

It's not necessarily their fault it's just our time in history where the world appears to be treading water while going somewhere, yet the destination of where that somewhere is, is anyone's guess. The world seems to be headed in a direction that is very unclear at the moment. And will remain unclear if two things continue as they are; our government continues within the framework that negates the Bible; and second, an arrangement of peace in the Middle East, especially over the ownership of Canaan, and the right to live must be established. After generations of trying to find solutions, it appears that a solution is not possible. Solutions, as many say, will only be accomplished when annihilation for the world is at hand. That seems to be the theology that both the Bible and the Quran are teaching. And that teaching requires the return of a Messiah.

Until, and unless those issues can be resolved, there will be no peace. And since the Bible tells us nothing is going to be settled until Christ comes to end the madness, there appears to be nothing we can do. In addition to the concerns discussed, we cannot omit Mother Nature from the equation of disrupting our peace of mind. Especially with the intensifying in fury and frequency bringing forth unprecedented disasters that are only going to escalate, that is if we can believe the Bible.

Add that to the debilitating influence Islam will continue having on our country, and a government that is opening our country to unprecedented times by allowing terrorist to establish a firm foothold. And then by aiding our enemies as the current leaders are doing, we have a world, and an America, that is "out of order." Perhaps we need to just hold tight to our sanity while riding out the storms that are coming.

Oh, don't think I didn't hear the minds of those who are saying, "We will be out of here before there are any storms." I, as well as every Christian who hears that theology hopes those who believe this teaching are right. If they are, then we, as born-again Christians, are right there with them. We're on the same team and on the same page. Therefore, when Christ returns, all born again believers are right there with those who belong to His family—no matter when He returns.

The longer He takes, the more Christians might have to face persecution, which just might be a continuing erosion of freedom and liberties. That absolutely will be the situation if either Islam or atheism win the battle for the soul of the world. But prior to that becoming a reality, Christ will come and put an end to the madness that will continue to escalate. A madness, if not a battle, of good versus evil that appears to be raging just beneath the surface of humanity. A time that seems to have arrived suddenly and unexpectedly. Signs of the last days that appear to be approaching much more rapidly than many would have surmised just a few short years ago.

Even now our freedoms are being taken away. The mask took away our expressions and the vaccine had the ability to take away our freedom. What many took away from those times was the ease in which the government, a handful of people, had such control over the lives of the American people. I don't think the antichrist will have any problem in taking control of this world considering the fear that emanated from the world during the latest pandemic.

Fear that was brought about by a world that doesn't realize fear is not of God. At least not the God as worshipped by Christians.

So many distractions that seem to be propelling us into a future while the destiny of that future is undefined. A destiny, for Christians at least, that appears to be coming. And, without the appearance of Christ, the future looks bleak for the Christian population. For those who resist the governments overreach with a mind-set that is contrary to Christians, a mindset defiant to the mind set of God, times could become stressful to say the least. The times Timothy Ware discussed earlier, and the times Patrick Heron warns us about when he says; we've been warned. By the signs of the times, "We've been warned."

Don't say it can't happen. Any conformer to laws and decrees that are against God's laws, i.e., abortion, same sex marriage, genocide, perhaps even gender change, will face persecution if they stand up and speak out. The voice of Christians will continue to be silenced while Islam will refuse to be silenced, as they have demonstrated. However, violence is not the way to peace, just as brutality is not the way to convert people.

Why can't Muslims see that? Perhaps they can but they, as we have seen, have an agenda. An agenda as Pastor John Hagee brought to our attention earlier. Remember, he said Islam must be victorious in accomplishing their agenda so not to prove Allah as a fabrication. The following information you might find interesting as it discusses some insight into the determination of Islam and why they want to dominate us.

the religion of submission

Many are saying these are interesting, maybe even exciting times to be alive—the times that appear to be close to the end. Since we as Christians, not Muslims, but Christians, have access to the knowledge of the times, we can know how the story ends by watching prophesy unfold. Perhaps the most important thing to take from this discussion is the "godlessness" and how "void" of the spirit is the religion of Islam.

Of course, Muslims would vehemently deny they lack the spirit of God, but then the question becomes "from which god do they receive inspiration?" The answer, as we know is Allah. They admit to that by rejecting the living God and accepting the spirit of Allah. Yet they consider anyone Islamophobic for even implying what has been mentioned. Am I wrong? Based upon the information establishing the root and the foundation upon which Islam was conceived, am I wrong in saying that they reject the living God and accept a fabricated one? If that is the situation, then am I wrong for saying they do not have the Spirit of God dwelling within them, and therefore are spiritless? Just saying.

I came across some information the other day you might find interesting as it sums up everything that has been said about Islam and the intention of those who follow Islam. The following is a letter that every American should consider before voting a Muslim of the Islamic faith to hold positions in our government. If one can read the following letter and still endorse a Muslim who puts Allah above America, its citizens, its way of life, and even above its God, then hope for America is a thing of the past. Many might even go so far as to say we have passed the point of retaining the country of our forefathers. Some might even say, we now owe our soul to the "angel of light." I believe it was Tennessee Ernie Ford some years ago who said in a song, "We owe our soul to the company store." And as George Carlin used to say, "We passed that place a long time ago."

Anyway, if you listen to the following letter, you will hear Islam saying, we will recite [the] Quran and say Allah-Hu-Akbar before beheading you. We will video tape those and send it to all infidels to watch. This was done in the Daniel Pearl situation. Remember, they sliced off his head and threw it on some bloody newspapers while they continued stabbing his lifeless body. At the same time, Muslims had dead American bodies hanging from bridges while dragging bloodied and beaten Americans through the streets for people to spit on. Yeah, these are great people we are allowing to run our country. As well as Berkeley students fund raising money to help them. I bet their parents are very proud.

Islam continues to tell us that before it is all over, we will surrender—ISLAM means surrender, [also, submission] to their authority. We will use your own values of kindness against you. You are destined to lose." Then he continues. "I was born and raised as Muslim. My whole family is still Muslim. I know every genetic code of Muslim. I know [the] Islamic brain. I live and breathe with them. I am an insider. I left Islam when I understood that Islam is a sick and evil religion."

I [Jason] got this post today, it is chilling and horrifying. What say you? PAY ATTENTION EVERYONE! Here is a post from a person that left Islam. SHA Resh Lamed Teresa Noliva and posted the following letter Wednesday, April 2016. You might find this interesting as well as very disturbing but again, we have been warned. Jason DeWitt posted a warning from an ex-Muslim. An insider, a person whose family remains Muslim. A warning that without a doubt should concern us all. Without concern, we as a country are lost.

The letter

"To the infidels of the West: The Constitution for the new Islamic Republics of EruoArabia and Amerislamia is under construction. We will fight the infidel to death. Meanwhile American laws will protect us. Democrats and Leftist will support us. N.G.O.s will legitimize us. C.A.I.R. will incubate us. The A.C.L.U. will empower us. Western Universities will educate us. Mosques will shelter us. O.P.E.C. will finance us. Hollywood will love us. Kofi Annan and most of the United Nations will cover our asses. Our children will immigrate from Pakistan, Egypt, Saudi Arabia, Iran, and Indonesia and even from India to the US and to the other Western countries. They will go to the West for education in full scholarship. America is paying and will continue to pay for our children's educations and their upbringing in state funded Islamic schools.

We will use your welfare system. Our children will also send money home while they are preparing for Jihad. We will take the advantage of American kindness, gullibility, and compassion, when time comes, we will stab them in the back. We will say one thing on the camera and teach another thing to our children at home. We will give subliminal messages to our children to uphold Islam at any cost. Our children in America will always care more about Islam Country's interest than US interest. We will teach our children Islamic supremacy from the very childhood.

We will teach them not to compromise with infidels. Once we do that from the very early age our children won't hesitate to be martyrs. We will take over the Europe first and then US will be next. We already have a solid ground in the UK, Holland, Sweden, Spain, Italy, Germany, and now in the US. Our children will marry Caucasian in Europe and in America. We will be mixed [mix] with [the] intricate fabric of the Western society but still will remember to Jihad when [the] time comes. Who are we? We are the 'sleeper cells.' We will raise our children to be loyal to Islam and Mohammad only. Everything else is secondary.

At the time of the real fight, we will hold our own children as our armor. When American or Israeli troops shoot at us the world will be watching. Imagine, the news in the world "Death of Muslim babies by infidels." We know CNN, ABC, CBS, and others are broadcasting this news live and condemning religion as the cause. Al-Jazeera will pour gasoline on the fire and the news will spread like wildfire. 'Americans killed 6 babies, 10 babies'…' 'Jews killed two more women.' Keep your Nukes in your curio cabinets. Keep your aircraft carrier or high-tech weaponry in the showcase. You cannot use them against us because of your own higher moral standard. We will take the advantage of your higher moral standard and use it against you. We will not hesitate to use our children as suicide bombers against you. Visualize the news flash all over the world, Muslim mother is sobbing...crying. ...Her babies are killed by Jews and Americans, while the whole world is watching live. Hundreds of millions of Muslims all around the world are boiling. They will march through Europe. We will use our women to produce more babies who will in turn be used as armor/shield. Our babies are the gift from Allah for Jihad. (Whoa, did not see that coming).

West manufactures their tanks in the factory. We will manufacture our military force by natural means by producing more babies. That is the way it is cheaper. You infidels at this site cannot defeat us. We are 1.2 billion. We will double again. Do you have enough bullets to kill us? On the camera: We will always say, 'Islam is the religion of Peace.' We will say, 'Jihad is actually inner Jihad.' Modern Muslim will say there is no link between Islam and Terrorism and the West will believe it because the West is so gullible. (Remember, they always say it is the "other guys" who are the bad Muslims—that is if they say anything).

Moderate Muslims all over the world will incubate Jihadist by their talk of defending Islam. Using the Western Legal system, we will assert our Sharia Laws, slowly but surely. We will increase in number. We will double again. You will be impressed when you meet a moderate Muslim personally. As your next-door neighbor, coworker, student, teacher, engineer, professionals you may even like us. You will find us well mannered, polite, humble that will make you say, 'wow'! (True, we saw that with Syed Farook and his wife, Tashfeen Malik when they shot those who threw them a bridal shower just days earlier).

He continues, Muslims are good and peaceful people, but we will stab you in your back when you are sleeping as we did on 9/11. There will be more 9/11 in Europe and in America. We will say, 'We do not support terrorism, but America got what it deserved.' Muslims CAIR, ISNA, MPAC and other international Islamic organization[s] will unite. We will partner with Leftist, ACLU, with Koffi Annan, and the UN, and Louis Farrakhan and, if we must, then even with France. Fasten your seatbelt. The war of civilizations has just begun.

A disturbing letter at best. Friends everything written in this book has been a result of what you just read. There is no hiding what Islam has planned for our country and unless we understand and recognize the source from where Islam gets its power, we will continue sliding down a very slippery slope. We can hope for the best, but considering Islamic determination for the last fourteen hundred years, and an enemy who is as smart and cunning as those just described by a former Muslim insider. Someone who put a price on his head by speaking out against the evils of Islam as he has. Many consider his description of Islam as the religion directed by the one referred to as the, "angel of light," or as others might say, "The Puppet Master of Islam."

We've been warned by someone in the know, someone who saw first-hand the evils from the inside and someone who knows how the brain of a Muslim works. Even those who we think are nice, they are still Muslim and have the same goals of all Muslims. And we are electing people who retain this mentality to help run our country. That bit of information proves we are lacking the understanding that they are here to destroy us as a country, and someday, because of this lack of understanding, they will pursue a path to see an Islamic flag flying over Washington.

No other group in history has had the determination to succeed as Islam, as well as the people who follow Islam. A fabricated religion brought forth by a night vision that produced a god diabolically opposed to the Creator God. A god with plans to destroy us as a Judeo-Christian nation along with all the infidels who live in that heathen nation referred to as the "Great Satan."

And all anyone can say to that is, "We've been warned. By the very word of God, we've been warned." This would be a good place to conclude but there is slightly more to say from some futurist preachers who have a few words to say to us regarding the current times and some coming times.

XXV

Post Letter Warnings

MANY BELIEVE 9/11 WAS ONE of the signs, perhaps even the first sign, that made us aware of such evil that currently exist in the world. Regarding 9/11, is there not a small bit of concern regarding Islam in your mind that didn't exist prior to 9/11? It was a very sad time for all Americans as well as Arab Americans. But just as importantly, it was a sad day for Middle Eastern American Christians as they were targeted for much abuse by a very hurt nation.

Our hearts went out to those Arab Americans, (Middle Eastern descendants) who were living in America and were subject to the abuse of a nation that was grieving. Grieving from a horrible atrocity imposed upon our nation by followers of Allah. You know, those the Berkeley students are raising money to help support their cause. Just when you think America could not get any dumber.

We know there are good Arab Americans who live among us, but again, the question becomes, how does one tell them apart? We just heard from one earlier by the name of Brigitte Gabriel, founder and president of <u>ACT! for America</u>. A Good Christian Arab American who lives among us, and sometimes unfortunately, they get thrown into the fray with Islamic Muslims who brought us 9/11. This happened after that horrendous occurrence, but again, how do we tell the good guys from the bad guys?

Simple, if they follow any God other than the creator God, the Judeo-Christian God, the God this country was founded upon, then their destiny is to kill in the name of the god, they serve. And that places them in the category of the "bad guys." But again, that is probably oversimplifying the matter. No matter how we try to justify it by perhaps over-compensating, we can never erase the blackest day in American history.

Now get this. Are you ready? You are not going to believe what you are about to read. Recently a school banned the colors of the American flag—red, white, and blue as inappropriate attire to be worn on 9/11 as it might offend Muslims. "It might offend Muslims!!!" How low can a country go in turning their back on what is America? What can someone be thinking who made that decision? Sometimes, the farther we go forward the farther back we seem to end up.

Once again, I must reiterate, how do we hold our head up as a country when an American school bans students from wearing red, white, and blue colors—colors that represent our flag, our country, our liberty, our independence, as well as an act that pays tribute to the families most affected on the infamous day of 9/11. Families, along with others who have lost loved ones over the years protecting this country. A country whose flag just happens to be red, white, and blue. 9/11 was a day among many that brought destruction directly to our country. To our county, and now BECAUSE Muslims might be OFFENDED, we withdraw from what is right and concede to what is wrong. Totally offensive to the America of our forefathers.

Americans should never forget it was the Muslim god, and those who support this Muslim god, that were responsible for the hurt Muslims brought to our country that infamous day. And if the truth be known, all Muslims serving Allah—and how can one be a Muslim without serving Allah, rejoiced over an event that saddened all Americans. But then, why not? After all, 9/11 advanced the cause of Islam and brought great grief to the nation Muslims refer to as, "The Great Satan." And as we know some of those who harbor this sentiment are now serving in our government and are responsible for our future. Only in America.

If that be the situation, then the question might become, how can they be trusted when they continue to promote Islam as a passive, nonaggressive, religion headed by diplomats who have our best interest at heart. And they label those who don't exactly see Islam through the lens of a Muslim as racist, or perhaps they consider them as Islamophobic. Those who differentiate the difference between the facts of Islam, rather than embrace words when all Americans know there are many individuals in the world of Muslim descent who would like to kill us by slicing our throat as they did with Daniel Pearl. But as you have probably noticed, Islam refers to those tragic moments as being perpetrated by the "other guys." The bad Muslims—the Islamic Avengers. As for the good guys, Islam is a "passive, maybe even a serene, religion.

The world religion

Many blame God for the current problems plaquing the world and maybe he is responsible for the conditions we are currently facing but perhaps there is a reason for this time in history. Many might say that the biggest disruption to the world has been God allowing the "angel of light," the nemesis of his to introduce Allah into the world. Why would God do that? Why would God create a nemesis that eventually He, God, was going to have to do battle with? Again, God knew exactly what He was doing. And He told us in advance what to look for as the end draws to a close.

By allowing Islam into the world, He knew the world would reach the place where the Seals of Revelation, especially the first four that are designed to remove peace from the world would be visibly discernible as many believe they are. But it isn't only Islam that is bringing trouble and turmoil to the world, we must contribute much of the current developments to a world controlled by Satan. I found the following information interesting regarding those who currently seem to be in control of the world, those we have been warned about, the spiritless ones. They seem to follow a godless path referred to as Humanism, Secularism, and New Agism.

The following are probably the best definitions of each. Karen Armstrong gives us a good description of a Christian's view relating to humanism in her book, *The History of God*. She says, "Humanism is a religion without God." Straight to the point. An Amazing Facts, Inc. pamphlet put it this way. "The age in which we live has normalized this false religion of self-worship. We even have a name for it—humanism." That is based upon the belief that man's reason (intellect) is sufficient to answer life's most profound questions, thus fulfilling the future needs, and that there is no God or moral absolutes. That is the belief that forms the axis of humanism. Many humanists define humanism as a religious movement. A religious movement void of any revelation of the existence of a Superior Creator, more of a "mind science" with the focus on intellect.

Here is how the New Agers take Humanism, basically, atheism, to an entirely different level. Those who believe in and follow New Age thinking have made their position quite clear regarding Christianity. The New Agers state their position very well when they say, "it is time to do away with 'the rotting corpse of Christianity' together with all its adjacent evils and misery and embrace the new faith of humanism." And considering what we know about humanism, those are rough words.

A secularist, as described by Bill O'Reilly, is someone who "believes there is no room for spirituality in the public arena, in the public debate policy arena. He or she rejects that this country was founded on Judeo-Christian philosophy and that this philosophy permeated our constitution. They reject that entirely, they say 'no, it's entirely man made, we don't base it on any philosophy other than what we feel is right for the occasion at the time.'"

If one considers a God capable of creating everything, a God who is all knowing, then everything being observed must be orchestrated with a cleverly defined ending in mind. Looking around and applying a little imagination and a lot of common sense, all the signs seem to be leading into the period of tribulation spoken of by the apostle John in the book of Revelation. I don't believe when looking around at the world today as opposed to the world twenty years ago, ten years ago, or even five years ago, one can deny that?

Many of today's preachers appear to be delivering the message that America, as well as the world in general, is continuing to head south rather quickly. It's almost as if the end times are knocking at our door and many cannot see them. And, if they see them, perhaps it is easier not to see them, as those times might involve hardships. It seems as if Islam, secularism, and the divisiveness of politics, will be on the minds of many for some time to come. Why is that?

Many believe that Muslims, and those politicians who are Muslim sympathizers serving in our government, will not stop at anything short of turning America into an Islamic country while at the same time the secularist seem to be hell bent on turning our country into a Socialist state. A country that is now referred to as garbage by Islam, and a country that appears to be controlled by anti-Christians. But once Islam takes over that will change according to them. According to them, Allah will bring light and understanding into the world. What a world we have become and what a world we are leaving our children and grandchildren.

That is if our children and grandchildren survive a world that is being plunged into the disarray that we are currently witnessing. Many remember when normality seemed to be the order of the day, now anything but normality exists. Islam seems to have been put on the back burner when, as many say, a dangerous bioweapon known as Corona virus was released upon the world. Indicating that, in addition to the dangers posed by Islam, many conclude that we are under attack by our own government.

A government that appears to be run by instructions from godless people, just saying. Those who accept laws and commands other than from God are godless. And that appears to be the mind-set of many in charge of making decisions that determine our future. At least until the coming of Christ, or al Mahdi, whoever comes first. Until then, their intentions never waver, they are going to continue pursuing a way of life that might be considered disruptive to the life of a conservative who would be more inclined to follow the principles of God.

However, having said that, if both Islam and Secularism have control of making decisions that affect our life—from the inside, thus advancing their agendas by gaining ground from the inside, as some have, then why blow up a building or two? Or down a plane or two? That seems to be where we are with Islam. And the moment is good, as Islam, rather than blowing up a building, they can pursue the path in the planning of another attack. And until then, they are content to work beneath the surface while planning our destruction. But in mentioning that, I am considered Islamophobic by many who say, why "rock the boat." It has been some time since Islam has raised its ugly head.

"Rocking the boat" as some might say invokes the worst of Islam as Islam besmirches those who bring information to the attention of others by bringing to the conversation such words as, uninformed, closed minded, fear monger, and even going so far as to deflect by bringing racist and bigotry into the conversation. And when all else fails they fall back on their go to word, "Islamophobia." Which is fine as it is their constitutional right to say those things. But through it all, the essence of what they mean comes through loud and clear. As if the letter earlier was not enough then how about another warning. This time from a Christian.

The Warning

Author Patrick Heron[53] talks about the book of Revelation when he says, "The book of Revelation has been sealed for centuries to almost everyone including most Bible-believing Christians. Now it is revealing itself to many people." That is true. We can see clearly, for the first time in history, the direction the world is heading from watching prophesy being fulfilled. And with a little foresight, one can see the culmination of events that have been leading us in that direction. Events that have been occurring for many years.

Patrick goes on to say that the events we are witnessing may be the final warning that God is giving people before his judgments come upon this earth. Giving people the final warning. Wow! Giving people the final warning. And he is not the only one who is bringing this message forward. Many who are speaking out are telling us that if the Bible is to be believed, then perhaps it is time to say, "We've been warned." By the signs of the times, "We've been warned."

Patrick Heron also brought us some more interesting information in his book *Apocalypse Soon* when he made several observations regarding the Bible's description of, not only the end times, but the events leading up to them. One chapter caught my attention, and that was Patrick's explanation of the Four Horsemen of the Apocalypse. He says the key to the closeness of the last days, or the closeness to the close of this age lies in Matthew 24:4–7. I found this to be true, as most of the futuristic pastors. Matthew Chapter 24 discusses much of the information contained in this book, and others, as it contains the words of Jesus describing the end of days.

The times to which Patrick alludes, seems to confirm these times of turmoil, as the times that are leading to the description

---

[53] Patrick Heron. *Apocalypse Soon.*

as found in the books of Revelation and Daniel. Times that are coming or the Bible is wrong. Maybe not tomorrow, but these times are coming. So assured of his convections, Patrick wrote:

> My wonderful wife Catherine and I have been married now for almost thirty years. She has given me three beautiful daughters for whom I would die. I am willing to stake my daughters' lives on the fact that the things that I discuss in this book will come to pass. I believe the events discussed will happen soon. I may be wrong in the soon part, but they will happen someday.

I, along with scores of others, seem to agree with Patrick. And that includes, Hal Lindsey, John Hagee, Mark Hitchcock, Jack Van Impe, Tim LaHaye, Dr. David Jeremiah, and Charles Stanley. They all appear to be saying the same thing. Therefore, if Patrick is wrong, then so are many others. But an unthinkable possibility could be that the Bible is wrong in describing the end of times. Both Patrick and millions of other Christians are banking on that not being the case.

The end is coming, and Christians are looking forward to that day, but they have no say and can do nothing to escalate the time. On the other hand, no other group in history has had the determination to succeed as Islam in bringing about the end. A fabricated religion brought forth by a night vision that produced a god, who, as we know, is diabolically opposed to the Creator God. A god with plans to destroy Americans, and America, as a Judeo-Christian nation. That is again, their destiny. And fulfilling Allah's desires is what Muslims live for. And all the infidels who live in that heathen nation referred to as the "Great Satan" must be eliminated. And all anyone can say to that is, "We've been warned. By the very word of God, the Bible, and the Qur'an, we've been warned."

The Terminal Generation

It appears, as mentioned, we are witnessing the time in history many have described as the end of the age or the "terminal generation." Both John Hagee and Tim LaHaye have indicated their belief that this is the last generation before the rapture, the coming of Christ for his family, his church. Really? Could this be the "terminal generation"—in other words, the last generation, or the generation to witness the commencement of events described within the Bible? We've already seen that Patrick Heron believes we could be the last generation. And John Hagee also believes we could be the terminal generation.

Others who believe we are living in the end times as mentioned include Tim LaHaye and Jerry Jenkins, as they write in their book, *Are We Living in the End Times*: "We believe 'this generation' [the terminal generation] refers to those alive in 1948." The year Israel became a State. Even Jack Van Impe gets in on it as he says Pope Francis will probably be the last Pope. How about that?

Could we be the last generation before the coming of Christ; the generation to see Christ coming to claim the Christians who have fallen asleep in him as well as those who are alive and appear to be awaiting his arrival? It appears time is running out on those who have been alive since 1948 to see the coming of Christ for his church. It could happen, but perhaps Tim and Jerry as well as John Hagee, were talking about those who would be alive to see the end of the age unfolding, as it appears to be. Thus, we will perhaps be the last generation before the Rapture or God's judgments begin to fall upon mankind, indicating some will begin to witness the signs of the times described in the Christian Bible, as the signs of the end and the nearness of His return.

A generation heading into the future with the opportunity to see the biblical end of the age as no generation before them. Nobody really knows for sure, but if we study the signs of the times, they say, the end is coming and "we have been warned." The signs of the times are such that those who believe Christ is ready to come for his church are probably looking upward as they say our redemption is near, meaning the rapture I assume, as some may be waiting for the time of the Second coming. And to my Christian friends who say the word rapture cannot be found in the Bible. I say, your right, but then neither can the word "Trinity" yet the understanding is there. I've never thought that argument against the theory of a Rapture ever held much water.

Let me ask a question. What do you think conjures up in the minds of those who are asked their thoughts about the "Last Days" or the "End Times"? There are probably several responses to that question; but the two major camps of thought I've run into seem to be the Christian camp, which mainly agrees that we could be either living in or approaching the last days as defined by the Bible.

The second camp, which is more secular in nature, respond with: "For as long as I can remember, people have been saying we are living in, or approaching, the last days or the end times." They both appear to be right. Ever since Jesus said, "Repent for the kingdom of Heaven is at hand" preachers have been preaching that message. And the pre-triber's are saying be ready because the kingdom of heaven is at hand as the signs of the times indicate. They could be right as the signs of the times signify; we could be closer than at any time anyone can remember.

We may not like some of the signs we are witnessing. Maybe a mandatory vaccination, or somethings equivalent. But as the terminal generation, we know these times lay before us. In the beginning proof of conformity may be a "vaccine passport" but eventually it will be a scannable device. A device that is not subject to getting lost, or forgotten, or stolen, and so on. But we know that. The Bible says, as Christians, we will know the signs of the end. Signs indicating just how close to the mark of the breast the world may be. And Islam will have a hand in our demise if we don't address the issue of electing Muslims to serve us. Especially when we know they only serve Allah.

That is seen as good in the eyes of many, Especially Islam, as the non-Christians, having a lack of spirit, places them with some of the same mentality that one could find in Islam. Basically, everything the unsaved world embrace that challenges the existence of the Christian God. Such as, including, but not limited to, horrendous acts such as abortions being acceptable, or gay marriages being acceptable, perhaps even gender identification. Of course, I describe the Secularist.

While that may be okey with many, others may find those actions are not acceptable to the God they honor. Or Islam, taking a license to advance their religion without regard to life or liberty. But the right to not exist has never entered my mind as I am betting it has never entered the mind of any Christian. Many would give up their life for the advancement of Christ, just as He did for us. Just as a Muslim would do the same for Allah. Does reconciliation sound like an unattainable, if not impossible, situation?

One last thought before moving on. Who would have believed we would ever be this close to a government of the people, by the people, and for the people, capable of mandating laws that go against a Christians' beliefs and Christian values? Even extending to denying that America is founded on Judeo-Christian values. Bill O'Reilly brought that bit of information to us earlier. Again, all signs pointing to the end of sanity as we know it. That could be how close we are to the identifying mark being imposed (mandated) by our government to buy and sell as described in Revelation.

If not this time, this pandemic, then when? Many put their money on the next pandemic that, according to them, is just around the corner. And with it comes the signs of the current era coming to an end just as the Bible has declared. Perhaps the most significant sign of, the beginning of the end, was the Jews returning to the land of Canaan. This momentous occurrence seemed to begin around the early part of 1900. Then at the end of the sixth-day war in 1967 Israel controlled Jerusalem. Two of the three most important events that must happen prior to the return of Jesus. I believe the third one was when Jerusalem become the capital of Israel. The place that king David claimed for the Jewish capital around ??????BC.

Those actions seem to be the last of the prophesies to be fulfilled before the return of Christ. Without either of those events occurring, the end could not come as described by the Christian Bible. While there have been many twists and turns in the history of the Jewish Nation, God kept them together through it all. And now, they are together in the place God has arranged so that His return is possible.

Speaking of Israel. From the very beginning when God chose them as His people, He has kept them together. Through adversities, including the holocaust, they have managed to remain a light on a hill forever shining brightly for the world to see. A light that has remained a constant reminder of God's presence and His power. From the very beginning, from Adam and Eve's son Seth, then through Noah's son Shem, then through Abraham, Isaac, and Jacob and their descendants, leading to the birth of Christ, the Jewish nation was formed and has remained in tack.

And through all the adversities that were a part of Jewish history for the past couple of thousand years the Jewish nation is still together, just as the Bible indicated they would be. That itself is a miracle. Then after all those years, beginning in the early part of the 20th century, the Jews began returning to the land promised to them by God. Thus, making His return imminent. How did that return of the Jews come about? But how did they manage to stay together as a nation for all these years? Especially after being scattered so many times. That was the question I Had. That might be an interesting topic to discuss before bringing this book to a close.

XXVI

The Reuniting of The Jews

WHETHER THE RETURNING OF THE Jews to their homeland at the beginning of the twentieth century and then becoming a state in 1948 has anything to do with end-time prophesy, I don't know, but it sounds very plausible. It is interesting listening to those who believe we could rapidly be approaching the days the Bible alludes to as "the last of days." Hal Lindsey in his book *The Late Great Planet Earth* confirms what he considers a very important end-time sign, as he says:

> I believe this generation is overlooking the most authentic voice of all, and that's the voice of the Hebrew prophets. They predicted that as man neared the end of history as we know it there would be a precise pattern of events that would loom up in history. Nations would fit into a certain pattern. And all of this would be around the most important sign of all—that is, the Jews returning to the land of Israel after thousands of years of being dispersed.

Israel, as Hal Lindsey put it in 1970, is the key to the last days. The remaining prophecies in the Bible could only be fulfilled with prophecies of the past being fulfilled. Future prophesies regarding Israel's prominence in the last days could only happen if the Jews occupied a State that up until 1948 did not exist. Or have control of the place where their coming Messiah will sit when he arrives, and that is Jerusalem, the city that was occupied by Muslims, but once again, fell under Jewish control during the 1967 conflict with the Muslims.

After 70 AD and prior to the early 1900's, there was no Israel as the Jews were scattered across the globe. The events being described in the Bible were viewed as impossible by many, especially in the book of Revelation, as there was no physical Israel to which the Bible kept eluding, only boundaries as defined by the Bible when the land of Canaan was promised to the Israelites. Not after AD 70 when Emperor Titus and his legions of Roman soldiers razed Israel, slaughtering hundreds of thousands of Jews and dispersing the rest to the slave markets of Egypt.

After being dispersed twice, once when Nebuchadnezzar destroyed the temple dispersing the people, and then again by Emperor Titus. Even after this, even after the ravages of King Nebuchadnezzar, Emperor Titus, and then Hitler, the people never wondered from the Creator God, the God of the Torah. They stayed with him, and he stayed with them. Even through it all, it didn't seem to deter the Israelites from trusting in God's promise of someday occupying the land of Canaan as their homeland and making the historical holy site of Jerusalem its Capital.

It was King David who some 3,000 years earlier dedicated Jerusalem to the Living God and established God's throne there for all eternity. It was former President Trump that re-established Jerusalem as Israel's Capital in 2017. An event that was necessary for end time prophesy to continue advancing towards the coming of Christ.

A lot of twist and turns throughout the centuries have taken place within the Israel community over the years. A designated people going from a scattered nation— twice, to returning to the land promised them by God in the Torah and as we recently witnessed, with the U.S. recognition of Jerusalem as the Capital of Israel, what more needs to be said.

Anyway, the importance of the information regarding the Jews returning to the Holy Land is not new. James Grant, an English Bible scholar writing in 1866 put it this way when he said, "the end will not take place until the Jews are restored to their own land and the enemies of Christ and the Jews have gathered together their armies from all parts of the Holy land, and the mustering and marshalling of these mighty armies, with a view to capturing Jerusalem must require a considerable time yet."[54]

This was written 40 years prior to the Jews being restored to their homeland, and 82 years before Israel was made a nation, and 104 years before writers like Hal Lindsey reemphasized the situation, and 140 years prior to the events taking place. But thousands of years prior to that, there were the prophets Ezekiel, Daniel, and Jeremiah, just to name a few, who were prophesying about these very events transpiring. For those who don't believe the Bible, explain that.

The Jewish Homecoming

In the early 1900s the Jews commenced the trek of "coming home," back to the land of Israel, as was prophesized several thousands of years earlier by Ezekiel and Jeremiah, and in 1948 they became a state, making future prophesy possible. Amazing! Simply amazing. Almost 1,900 years after the Jews were deposed from Israel and 2,440 years after the prophet Daniel said they would return, they returned to make the land of Canaan their permanent home. Sounds like a very important event of prophesy being brought to our attention. The Bible conveys to us information that says the Jews will be occupying the land promised to them by God when He returns. That is a promise of God. That is in the Bible.

---

[54] Walter Martin's book, *Kingdom of the Cults.*

Since it was prophesied, the Jews would return to and occupy the land of Canaan prior to the coming of Christ, they had to have control of Jerusalem, Of course, that is the Christian view. As for the Jews they have not accepting Christ as the Messiah, and will be preparing the way for their Messiah, as an awareness of Christ has not yet come to them. But that doesn't matter, Jerusalem must be under the control of the Israelites and that happened during the sixth-day war in 1967 when they wrestled control away from the Muslims.

Interesting information. While biblical scholars have been telling us of the return of the Jews and the reestablishment of a Jewish state for hundreds of years as a necessity of biblical prophecy to be fulfilled, it might be somewhat interesting to see just what transpired in history to allow, perhaps even stimulate, maybe even excite the Jews to begin the pilgrimage of "coming home"— coming home to the land promised by God to Abraham and handed down through the descendants of Abraham beginning with the patriarchs, Isaac, and Jacob, whose linage brought forth the legendary twelve tribes of Israel. The following information is provided by John Hagee in one of his books. At least, that is where I came across it. The information seems to establish the ownership of Canaan without any questionable areas of doubt.

Upon coming home, the land of Canaan was once again the homeland of the Jews with designated boarders. It was as if someone knew the Bible. What made everything possible has become known as the Balfour Declaration. An agreement that allocated the land of Canaan to the Jewish people and it was that agreement that make the return possible. Though it went through several drafts, the final version was issued on November 2, 1917, in a letter from Balfour to Lord Rothschild, president of the British Zionist Federation returning the land of Canaan to the Jews, thus fulfilling biblical prophecy.

The essence of the agreement was in World War I; the British were cut off from their source to make cordite gunpowder.

First Lord of the Admiralty Winston Churchill went to Chaim Weizmann, a Jewish chemist, and asked him if he would find a way to make several tons of synthetic gunpowder. Without it, bullets couldn't be fired, artillery was useless, and cannons on ships were mere ornaments. The outcome of the war was at stake.

Weizmann and his associates discovered how to make a massive amount of synthetic gunpowder within weeks. Thus, the Jewish inventor played a major role in the victory of WWI over Germany. In thanking Chaim Weizmann, the Balfour Declaration was implemented, which allowed the Jews to return to the land promised them. After the war, Lord Balfour asked Chaim Weizmann what England could do to honor him. Weizmann asked that his people be given a homeland. Lord Balfour created an historical document known to this day as the "Balfour Declaration."

A document giving the Jewish people what God had already promised them in the book of Genesis several thousands of years earlier—a homeland. (Genesis 15:7-8). As a matter of fact, it was at the time God visited Abraham and told him he was going to inherit the land of Canaan that Abraham became skeptical, but God assured him by entering a blood covenant with him to show just how serious He was. Also, dropping down to verse 13 we learn about the captivity of the Nation of Israel for 400 years by the Egyptians. An event that didn't transpire for thousands of years after it was prophesied.

The Jews returned to the land that had been promised to them thousands of years earlier. And that is after being rousted twice before, and even enduring the onslaught of Hitler's gas chambers. Then for the last time in the early 1900's the Jews came home. As I was typing that I was wondering what Bill Maher and Jillette Penn would have to say about the Jews returning as had been predicted thousands of years earlier from a book they think is fiction. Coincidence? Serendipity? Perhaps.

Right before our very eyes, the moment of the Balfour Declaration, it appears that a gigantic piece of Bible prophesy was being fulfilled. The Jews were now, once again, in possession of the promised land of Canaan, and in 1948 those descendants of Seth and Shem and Abraham, Isaac, and Jacob made the land of Canaan a Jewish State, a state dedicated to God. When President Truman indicated, he was going to support Israel's statehood, America was the only country to stand with Israel at that time. Truman took this stand even when his advisors warned against it as they said it would upset the Muslim population—it did, and still does. And as they say the rest is history. Then when President Trump relocated the U.S. Embassy, recognizing Jerusalem as Israel's capital, as we know, that set Islam's hair on fire.

It appears from the information covered so far that the ownership of the land of Canaan would be settled. Most might be inclined to concede the ownership of the parcel of land being discussed should have ended with the Balfour Declaration, which, as we have seen, gives the land occupied by Israel to the Jews in the eyes of many. At least it should but as we know it doesn't.

Otherwise, we would not be repeating how Israel must be destroyed, and the land of Canaan returned to the descendants of Ishmael and Esau. Descendants from the linage of Ham and Japheth, two sons of Noah's leading to Abraham which as we know is entirely different from the linage of Abraham, Isaac, and Jacob with linage traceable back to Shem. From this information it appears the dispute for the land of Canaan is a family dispute, but then when Allah entered the picture the anger became directed at anyone who favors Israel over Islam. And the Jewish God over the Islamic god.

Think about what is being said by Islam, there is no other way to eliminate the God of Israel and retake the land of Canaan other than to push Israel into the sea, which is the goal of Allah thus destroying the people called by the Creator God and referred to as "his elect." I believe we just agitate them because we support the God of Israel. By eliminating everybody and everything that is not Islamic, they are fulfilling their destiny. They are preparing the world for returning the throne of David, the throne designated for Christ to its rightful owner—Allah. To them al Mahdi the coming Messiah who is answerable to Allah who is answerable to the "angel of light" will return when the world is ready to accept him, and he will reign from David's throne in Jerusalem.

Don't forget if Israel is eliminated there will be no more Christian God. As we know by our knowledge of the Bible, Israel must remain exactly where they are and the God of Christians will remain as the everlasting living God, so in the end, Allah loses. I say that from believing our God can beat up your god, or as the Bible indicates He will be triumphal over all gods who come against Him.

But that is no victory for Christians who are enduring the persecution that Islam can force upon them. Persecution as in losing their jobs, having to conform to their religion, or take a chance on being sued, and so on. But the good news is we have many experts who are warning us of the current times and making sure Christians are aware of the signs of the end, as well as pointing out, just how close to the end we could possibly be. Wow! Where does one go after reading that? And considering everything else that has been brought to our attention, is anyone still on the fence as to Islamic intent? Or the Secularist intent as well? If so, then nothing more can be said. With that we just wait for the other shoe to fall. And with that, I would like to conclude with some parting words.

XXVII

Some Parting Words

I HAVE SAID WHAT I have said as my friends would say, "to say this." Jay Sekulow gave us some serious information regarding Islam. He told us that Shiite Muslims believe Jesus will return and assist the Mahdi to convert the world to Shiite Islam. He also told us that terrorists burn entire villages to the ground with the children's wailing heard miles away while Christian men are forced to kneel above explosives that are detonated by jihadists.

Jay also said that upon familiarizing ourselves with fanatical Islam, we find they are rewarded for blowing themselves up while killing infidels. Then there are honor killings. Every year many women are killed in the name of preserving the family honor. And according to Jay Sekulow[55] their offenses include dating without the family's approval, marrying a non-Muslim, or having an extramarital affair. Jay also tells that, "Islam teaches that the blood of infidels is not equal to the blood of Muslims and commands them to treat non-Muslims harshly and fellow Muslims mercifully."

I said that to say this. Jay told us the reason he wrote his book was to convey the message that if we don't act soon, then the world as we know it could cease to exist. And he wrote that prior to Covid and the toll that pandemic took upon all Americans. It seemed as if America has been left with more questions than answers. That just emphasizes the importance of knowledge in these last days. Knowledge and wisdom, both of which comes from the Holy Spirit. Followers of Jesus will understand what Jay

---

[55] Jay Sekulow's book *Unholy Alliance*.

meant. Not everyone will. It is as if history is writing itself and it is pursuing the path of *the* many. The question is, "are *the* many leading us to the place that excludes God?"

As this era draws to a close, we may have to suffer the persecution that prevailed during the early church, as well as the persecution witnessed during the days of the reformers, which may include death. Regarding this death, as mentioned, it is the first death, the physical death that everyone will have to endure. But Christ has told us not to have any fear of that death as that is not the death that separates us from Him. It is the second death, known as the spiritual death, and as every Christian knows, that is the death we must fear.

Some time back (1995) Peter and Paul Lalond wrote a book title; "*Mark of the Beast*" wherein they wrote that it doesn't take a handful of PhDs to see the direction the world is headed. They say, "the return of Christ is very near. This faith and this great hope are not built on a few random and isolated prophecies…It is built simply on reading the word of God and then looking at all the major news events of the day…you don't need a handful of PhDs to do that." Wow! How right they were then, and how right they are now. And that was in 1995. Look how the times have changed.

During the writing of their book, they had no idea of the Corona Virus that was going to send shock waves around the world bringing us to the place we currently find ourselves. Somewhat waiting for the next shoe to fall. As for Peter and Paul, they could only imagine these current times from reading the Bible. The many concerns we are dealing with now were not even imagined in 1995. Maybe it's time to start seriously looking for the safety of Noah's ark, and inviting others to join us in that ark as well, because some serious storms may be headed our way.

Those around to witness the return of Christ in the "not so distant future," may be considered by many experts to be the "Terminal Generation" as discussed earlier. A time brought to our attention by reading the word and then looking at the current worldly conditions. Conditions that Peter and Paul could only imagine. And let us not forget what author Patrick Heron said in his previously mentioned book *Apocalypse Soon*: "The book of Revelation has been sealed but now, more than ever, it is being opened and revealed for all to see." He also said he believed that God is giving people one last chance to get into the ark of safety before the judgments of God, as revealed in the Book of Revelation, begin to fall on the earth." While we have heard those words before, they seem worthy of repeating.

Tim LaHaye and Ed Hindson wrote a book some time back titled *"Global Warning"* (not global warming) where-in they (as well as many others) seem to be screaming to get our attention about the current times. The reason I bring up their book once again is to repeat their answer when asked the question; How close are we to the end? They said, "There is no doubt that we are fast approaching the final chapter of human history. The hoof beats of the Four Horsemen of the Apocalypse can be heard in the distance. The stage is set for the final acts of the human drama."

The book of Matthew tells us the destruction defined in Revelation is destined to happen. When we see these things coming to past we are not to be alarmed as these things must come to past before the era draws to a close. Upon this knowledge, perhaps, as Patrick says, God is giving people one last chance before His judgments commence. Meaning turning to Him and relying on Him above everything else. Okay, sounds plausible. But without the security of material things including money, or as some say "the security of gold" while others may even be touting the benefits of Crypto currency as the currency of the future.

As every Christian knows and promotes, nothing will take the place of security like trusting in God. Some may find the acceptance of "only Christ" a bit hard to convince the mind that trusting in what Bill Maher considers an imaginary friend is the only way to find peace, hope, and a harmonious feeling of completeness. I've heard many say they like themselves much better after accepting Christ. Many express they like who they have become after realizing it is "only Christ that has the answers"— and then relying upon that as a truism by faith. It is that theology that will help Christians endure the coming times. At least until the Rapture.

The sad part of the times we are living in, the times described by the Bible as perhaps the coming times—equating them to "birth pains," many people are oblivious to the future as they are not even aware of the pending tribulation that has been slated to be unleashed upon the world in the last days. Many don't find any alarm in the coming times, but many do. For those who do— mainly those who acknowledge future horizons and yet approach them with cautious optimism, the future will not catch them off guard. As Dr. Martin Luther King, Jr., once said, "If you knew the world was going to end tomorrow, plant a tree today." There isn't anything anyone can do to stop what has been preordained (predestined, prophesied) to happen, we can only be advised and pass the word to others.

If only we could return to the years prior to 9/11. The years prior to the violence of MS-13. The years prior to the refugee problems. The years prior to the opioid epidemic and the times prior to playing whack-a-mole with Islamic terrorist, and the times before killing and mocking and disrespecting policemen became the thing to do to emphasis one's displeasure. The time before Antifa, and BLM, and political malfunctions that have been witnessed over many years by both the right and the left. Not one party, or individual, could have brought us to the place in time we seem to find ourselves. A time where hate and disrespect have become so obvious it appears to have entered the very soul of America. An America Peter and Paul never saw, and yet warned us about.

Without being apathic it appears the world is headed in a direction that was predicted over two thousand years ago, And, amazingly, we have arrived. There have been hundreds of preachers and thousands of books written by futurist telling us the exact same thing. And the preaching on this subject seems to be getting more pronounced with each passing year. Because of this, I am saying the same thing as Jay Sekulow wrote in this book, as well as Joel Richardson, who wrote about when he wrote the book, The Islamic Antichrist.

We have an enemy, well actually two, that are destined to change our way of life, atheism that shows up in the form of secularism, and the religion of Islam. Even Hank Hanegraaff says, "to misapprehend the facts in an age of Islamic terrorism and expansionism is a price no one can afford to pay." And to miscalculate the facts in an age of secularism is also a price one cannot afford to pay as well.

To many the question may be, "And this is our future? While it is the destiny of Muslims who follow Allah to destroy America, I believe Satan is way ahead of them from another direction. It's obvious there are many powers vying for control of the world, as well as for control of our minds, or the world would not be as messed up as it is. Serendipity powers? Spiritual powers? Atheist powers? Perhaps, even Godly powers. What is behind the turmoil? We have learned from history, and from Nebuchadnezzar's dream, that all great empires at some point seem to meet their waterloo. And the culprit for America is corruption and greed and that unquenchable thirst for power, and a government, for the most part, run by people who seem to be lacking the Spirit of God, that is our waterloo. That is what the Secularist world offers.

When it comes to last day Islamic theology, there appears to be no grey area, no in-between, no compromise, not even any negotiation. Allah, the god introduced into the world by the "angel of light" and brought forth by Muhammad's vision, a vision that introduced a fabricated god to a distinct group of people to follow and claim as their own. A god that must reign supreme, and everyone who doesn't accept Allah as their god or bow to the coming Islamic Messiah must be "eliminated"—by Jesus. Wow!

And that my friend, as most Christians would probably say, is not seeing eye to eye.

If you are reading this last paragraph, then thanks for hanging in there. It took many years to compile the information necessary to write this book and seeing the finished product, I can only say that I am quite proud of what God has allowed me to accomplish. All credit goes to Him. If you disagree with anything written, then take it up with Him. But then I jest.

We both know that it would be impossible to agree upon everything, but we as Christians can agree upon the most import part of being a Christian. What would you say that might be? The knowledge of living forever while having fun seems to work for me. We are going to be together for eternity to pursue a life that cannot even be described. And with that knowledge, most Christians would probably say, "It truly does not get any better that that." And as Jesus might say, "have a great day and don't forget to hug someone, especially your children."